INDIAN MENU PLANNER

ISBN: 185 605 3776

Published by **Blitz Editions**
an imprint of
Bookmart Limited
Registered Number 2372865
Trading as Bookmart Limited
Desford Road
Enderby, Leicester, LE9 5AD

Conceived and designed by
Pramod Kapoor
at
Roli CAD Centre

Photographs:
Dheeraj Paul
Neeraj Paul
Deepak Budhraja

Production:
Naresh Nigam
Abhijit Raha

Typesetting:
Naresh L. Mondal

Text Editor:
Lavinia Rao

Printed and bound at
Star Standard Industries Pte. Ltd., Singapore

INDIAN MENU PLANNER

Blitz Editions

Acknowledgement

The publisher would like to thank the **New Delhi Hilton** and **The Ashok Group of Hotels,** New Delhi for making available the kitchens of their restaurants for the photography and preparation.

Grateful thanks to Madhu Arora, Kiran Kapoor and Mili Paul for the help they have given in bringing out this book.

Contents

Introduction 7

Chicken
Lamb
Fish & Seafood

Vegetarian
Accompaniments
Desserts

The Recipes 8-103

Basic Recipes 104

Suggested Menus 108
Index 111

INTRODUCTION

In a land so rich in tradition which has seen the rise of so many civilizations, it would be surprising if Indian food had remained untouched by the hands of history. The ancient Indians were a wheat-eating race and gave the world that essentially Indian bread, the *chapati* (a small, flat thin cake of unleavened whole meal bread). The Mughals made a culinary coup by bringing in the *tandoor* (an oven made of earth and heated by a slow charcoal fire) and creating the delectable Mughlai cuisine of *biryanis* (an exquisite rice preparation with meat, herbs and seasonings) and *kormas* (a spicy meat or vegetable preparation). The British *raj* spawned an interesting Anglo-Indian gastronomic culture of which the *jhaal frezi* (stir fried vegetables or meat cooked with onions and chillies) and the mulligatawny soup (a soup made of lentils, meat pieces and rice) are still eaten with relish.

This book gives one hundred thousand exciting Indian menus to choose from. In a rather novel way, it helps the reader to make as many permutations and combinations as he or she wants. The recipe pages are sliced into three: starters, main courses and desserts and every dish is illustrated. The time required to prepare each dish is marked by coloured bands. If one wishes to create one's own menu for a special meal, all one has to do is choose a starter from one page and the main course and dessert from another using the time bands.

Indian food gets its characteristic taste, subtlety and aroma from the country's vast reservoir of spices. The recipes for preparing spices from the abundant tropical herbs and the manner in which they are to be mixed during cooking too have been handed down by tradition. This book gives the reader a thorough idea of the spices and garnishing required in each dish alongwith the recipes. Apart from adding that very special quality to a cuisine which is the legacy of a glorious past, spices have medicinal and preservative properties. *Lal mirch* (red chilli powder) gives the food a sharp, hot flavour, *haldi* (turmeric) not only adds colour but also helps in digestion, *jeera* (cumin) imparts fragrance while a pinch of *heeng* (asafoetida) gives a unique taste to the food and acts as an excellent preservative.

The variety and range of Indian food can amaze any cuisine connoisseur. Food is different in every region of India, and this book attempts to cover this range by giving recipes for preparations as exotic as lotus stem curry and as inviting as chicken almond steak. In a sub-continent of such vast dimensions, food and climatic influence have to be closely inter-related. In Kashmir, everyone eats a lot of meat as the weather is very cold. The cold climate there helps in the farming of saffron, and food seasoned with saffron keeps the body warm. In the dry desert land of Rajasthan, *chapatis* made of millet accompanied with red chillies are eaten with great gusto as they help the body retain water. Pepper is an important ingredient in the food from Kerala as the humidity in the air helps in its cultivation. While the east of India prefers to cook their fish in mustard oil, in the south coconut oil is the medium of cooking as the wet climate favours the luxuriant growth of coconut trees.

There are a wide range of cooking styles used in the preparation of Indian food. *Dum Pukht*, which entered the country from the north-west frontier, is a way in which food is cooked over a slow charcoal fire in the *tandoor* so that it can mature in its own juices and the various spices added to it. Deep frying in a *kadhai* (wok), stir frying on a *tawa* (griddle) and using the traditional *handi* (pot) are the other methods commonly used.

The presentation of an Indian meal is as important as the actual process of cooking. Food is served in different regions in different ways. In north India, meals are served in a *thali* (a large round plate with raised sides made of steel or silver and sometimes even gold), and in the south the banana leaf is usually used to serve food. So begin your gastronomic odyssey and see how many exotic meals you can serve.

Cold Cucumber Soup

Ingredients

Cucumber, quartered alongwith peel 1 kg
Butter 25 gms / 5 tsp
Onions, quartered 200 gms / 1 cup
Vegetable stock, strained 2 litres / 10 cups
Salt to taste
White pepper powder 3 gms / ½ tsp
Cream, whipped 100 gms / ½ cup

Method

1 Heat butter in a pot, add onions and sauté till transparent, add the cucumber and sauté for a few minutes.

2 Stir in the vegetable stock, salt to taste and white pepper powder. Cover and cook on low heat for 20-25 minutes till the cucumber is cooked and tender. Stir in the cream, remove from heat and allow to cool.

3 Blend the soup to obtain a purée and strain through a muslin cloth.

4 Transfer to a soup bowl and refrigerate for 1 hour.

5 Serve chilled, garnished with cream.

Chicken in a Flavoured Gravy

Ingredients

Chicken thighs, boneless 800 gms
Green cardamoms *(choti elaichi)* 4
Chicken stock ½ litre / 2½ cups
Cinnamon *(daalchini)* 1" stick
Cloves *(laung)* 10
Garlic paste (page 105) 20 gms / 4 tsp
Garlic, chopped 30 gms / 2 tbs
Ginger paste (page 105) 20 gms / 4 tsp
Onions, sliced 90 gms / 6 tbs
Refined oil 75 ml / 5 tbs
Saffron a few strands
Salt to taste
Yellow chilli powder 3 gms / ½ tsp

Method

1 Cut chicken into bite-sized pieces. Soak saffron in a little water in a spoon for 10 minutes. Crush and keep aside.

2 Heat oil in a saucepan and add chopped garlic. Sauté till brown. Add the onions and sauté till light brown. Add cinnamon, cloves and cardamoms and sauté till the onions turn golden brown.

3 Add the ginger and garlic pastes, chicken, salt and yellow chilli powder. Stir for 3-4 minutes. Add chicken stock and bring to boil. Cover and simmer till chicken is tender.

4 Remove from fire. Take out the chicken pieces from the gravy. Strain the gravy into another pot through a soup strainer.

5 Cook the gravy till reduced to a sauce-like consistency. Add the chicken pieces and cook for a minute.

6 Stir in the prepared saffron and serve hot, accompanied by an Indian bread of your choice

Broccoli and Carrot Pulao

Ingredients

Rice, basmati 400 gms / 2 cups
Broccoli, (small flowerets) 150 gms / ¾ cup
Carrots, diced, parboiled 100 gms / ½ cup
Oil 30 ml / 2 tbs
Cumin *(jeera)* seeds 8 gms / 1½ tsp
Bayleaf *(tej patta)* 1
Cloves *(laung)* 3
Black peppercorns 5 gms / 1 tsp
Salt to taste
Water 1 litre / 6 cups

Method

1 Clean, wash and soak the rice in water for 10 minutes. Drain and keep aside.

2 Heat oil in a heavy bottomed pan, sauté cumin seeds, bay leaf, cloves, and black peppercorns till they crackle. Add the carrots, broccoli and salt, stir-fry for 3-4 minutes.

3 Remove and discard whole spices, keep the vegetables aside.

4 Boil water in a separate pot, cook the rice until done and drain excess water.

5 Gently fold in the cooked vegetables into the rice, transfer to a serving platter. Serve hot, accompanied by Walnut Raita (page 98).

Minced Peas and Potatoes 98
Mint Chutney 102
Mint Raita 94
Mixed Vegetable Raita 94
Moong Daal Halwa 76
Mushroom and Corn Bonanza 84
Mushrooms in Tomato Gravy 88
Mushroom Pulao 20
Mustard flavoured Fish Curry 72

N

Naan 34

O

Orange Raita 98

P

Pickle Lamb Curry 50
Pomegranate Chicken 18
Pomegranate Potatoes 100
Poori 24
Potato Baskets 90
Potato Curry 90
Potatoes in Chutney 88
Prawn Biryani 16
Prawn Curry 66
Prawn Cutlets 60

R

Rabari 88
Rajbhog 56
Ras Malai 52
Rasgoola 54

S

Saunth 102
Sesame Prawn Tikka 58
Shahi Tukda Nawabi 66
Shrimps in Coconut 60
Slow oven Chicken with a hint of Fenugreek 32
Slow Oven Tandoori Chicken 30
Spiced Cauliflower 94
Spicy Lamb Chops 40
Spicy Lamb Leg 56
Spinach Soup 12
Steamed Savory Gramflour Dish 72
Stir Fried Chicken 26
Stir-fried Chicken with Spring Onions 24
Stir-fried Lamb Delight 46
Stir-fried Mushrooms 86
Stuffed Chicken Steaks 40
Stuffed Cottage Cheese Tikka 84
Stuffed Parantha 36
Stuffed Potato Cutlets 76

T

Taftan 30
Tandoori Chicken 28
Tandoori Chicken Chaat 42
Tandoori Lobster 68
Tandoori Prawns 64
Tandoori Roti 38
Tandoori Salad 70
Tangy Aubergines 102
Tangy Chicken 34
Tangy Gramflour Curry 46
Tangy Lentil Soup 48
Tangy Yoghurt Soup 18
Tomato and Coconut Soup 16
Tomato and Coriander Soup 20
Tomato Chutney 100
Tomato flavoured Chicken 12
Tomatoes stuffed with Mushrooms 92

W

Walnut Raita 98

Y

Yam Kabab 96
Yellow Chutney 102
Yellow Daal 42
Yoghurt flavoured Cottage Cheese Cutlets 100
Yoghurt flavoured Lamb Kabab 54

INDEX

A

Assorted Fritters 98

B

Bakarkhani 26
Barbecued Chicken Drumsticks 22
Barbecued Lamb Cubes 52
Barbecued Liver 56
Batter coated stuffed Tomatoes 94
Besan Ladoo 68
Boondi Raita 96
Broccoli and Carrot Pulao 8

C

Carrot and Orange Soup 14
Cauliflower Kabab 78
Chenna Payas 58
Chicken Almond Steaks 16
Chicken Kabab 38
Chicken Biryani 14
Chicken in a flavoured Gravy 8
Chicken in a rich creamy Gravy 22
Chicken Kababs with Nuts 36
Chicken Seekh Kabab 28
Chicken Spring Rolls 32
Chicken Tikka 24
Chicken with Black Pepper 20
Chicken with Spinach 10
Chutney Fish Tikka 66
Cocktail Kababs 48
Coconut Burfee 72
Coconut Chutney 100
Cold Cucumber Soup 8
Colourful Chicken Seekh Kabab 30
Cottage Cheese and Capsicum Delight 78
Cottage Cheese Croquettes 82
Cottage Cheese cooked in a Wok 82
Cottage Cheese Pulao 22
Cottage Cheese Seekh Kabab 86
Cottage Cheese Tikka 80
Crispy Cauliflower 96
Crispy Lentil Strips 102
Crunchy Okra 92

D

Daal Makhani 40
Daal Panchmela 44
Dahi Bhalla 92

E

Egg and Cheese coated Chicken Legs 34
Exotic Chicken Dumplings 14
Exotic Lamb Kababs 46
Exotic Lamb Soup 10

F

Falooda 82
Fennel flavoured Prawns 62
Fenugreek flavoured, Grilled Lamb Cubes 50
Fenugreek flavoured Prawns 58
Fish Kababs 64
Fish Moilee 74
Fish Rolls 76
Fish Rolls stuffed with Prawns 68
Fish Tikka 62

G

Gajrela 74
Ginger Chicken Kababs 26
Ginger Lamb Chops 38
Goan Fish Curry 70
Gobi Musallam 94
Gosht Shahi Korma 53
Gramflour Pancakes 74
Gulab Jamum 50

I

Imarti 62

J

Jackfruit Pulao 18

K

Kesar Sandesh 70
Khameeri Roti 28
Khasta Roti 86
Kheer 78
Kujja Kulfi 84
Kulfi 82

L

Lachha Parantha 32
Lamb Biryani 10
Lamb cooked in rare Spices 48
Lamb cooked in whole Spices 44
Lamb Curry 52
Lamb Seekh Kabab 44
Lamb Shanks in Gravy 54
Lamb stir-cooked in a Spicy Gravy 42
Lavang Latika 60
Lemon Rice 12
Lotus Stems in an Exotic Curry 80

M

Makhana ki Kheer 90
Malpua 64
Mango Kulfi 80
Minced Lamb with Peas 36

Celebration

Soup
- Exotic Lamb Soup 10

Starters
- Lamb Seekh Kabab 44
- Potato Baskets 90

Main Course
- Tomato flavoured Chicken 12
- Cottage Cheese cooked in a Wok 82
- Lamb cooked in whole Spices 44

Accompaniments
- Daal Makhni 40
- Lamb Biryani 10
- Tandoori Roti 38
- Naan 34
- Mixed Vegetable Raita 94

Desserts
- Makhana ki Kheer 90
- Kujja Kulfi 84

Soup
- Cold Cucumber Soup 8

Starters
- Tandoori Chicken 28
- Ginger Chicken Kababs 26

Main Course
- Potatoes in Chutney 88
- Chicken Almond Steaks 16
- Stir-Fried Mushrooms 86

Accompaniments
- Daal Panchmela 44
- Chicken Biryani 14
- Bakarkhani 26
- Naan 34
- Walnut Raita 98
- Mint Chutney 102

Desserts
- Chenna Payas 58
- Rasgoola 54

Starters
- Sesame Prawn Tikka 58
- Barbecued Liver 56
- Tandoori Lobster 68

Main Course
- Pickled Lamb Curry 50
- Chicken with Spinach 10
- Lotus Stems in an Exotic Curry 80

Accompaniments
- Mushroom Pulao 20
- Tandoori Roti 38
- Khasta Roti 86
- Boondi Raita 96

Desserts
- Ras Malai 52
- Lavang Latika 60

Soup
- Tomato and Coriander Soup 20

Starters
- Yoghurt flavoured Lamb Kabab 54
- Barbecued Chicken Drumsticks 22

Main Course
- Lamb Shanks in Gravy 54
- Fish Rolls 76
- Shrimps in Coconut 60
- Spiced Cauliflower 94

Accompaniments
- Khameeri Roti 28
- Tandoori Roti 38
- Cottage Cheese Pulao 22

Desserts
- Lavang Latika 60
- Rice Kheer 78

Starters
- Ginger Lamb Chops 38
- Cocktail Kababs 48
- Fish Tikka 62

Main Course
- Exotic Chicken Dumplings 14
- Spicy Lamb Leg 56
- Goan Prawn Curry 66

Accompaniments
- Tandoori Roti 38
- Lachha Parantha 32
- Mushroom Pulao 20
- Dahi Bhalla 92

Desserts
- Lavang Latika 60
- Malpua 78

For vegetarian

Starters
- Cottage Cheese Tikka 80
- Stuffed Potato Cutlets 76

Main Course
- Minced peas with Potatoes 98
- Mushroom and Corn Bonanza 84
- Tangy Aubergines 102

Accompaniments
- Cottage Cheese Pulao 22
- Lachha Parantha 32
- Mixed Vegetable Raita 94

Desserts
- Gajrela 74
- Malpua 64

Quick & Easy

Soup
Tangy Yoghurt Soup 18
Starter
Tandoori Chicken Chaat 42
Main course
Potato Curry 90
Shrimps in Coconut 60
Accompaniments
Poori 24
Broccoli and Carrot Pulao 8
Dessert
Moong Daal Halwa 76

Soup
Cold cucumber soup 8
Starters
Gramflour Pancakes 74
Potato Baskets 90
Main Course
Tangy Chicken 34
Fenugreek flavoured prawns 62
Accompaniments
Khasta Roti 86
Mint Raita 94
Dessert
Rabari 88

Soup
Tomato and Coconut Soup 16

Starter
Assorted Fritters 98
Main Course
Minced Peas and Potatoes 98
Chicken in a Rich Creamy Gravy 22
Accompaniments
Khameeri Roti 28
Mushroom Pulao 20
Dessert
Shahi Tukda Nawabi 66

Starter
Crispy Lentil Strips 102
Yam Kabab 96
Main Course
Pomegranate Chicken 18
Accompaniments
Daal Panchmela 44

Khasta Roti 86
Tomato Chutney 100
Orange Raita 98

Soup
Tomato and Coriander Soup 20
Main Course
Crispy Cauliflower 96
Lamb Stir-cooked in a Spicy Gravy 42
Accompaniments
Yellow Daal 42
Khameeri Roti 28
Dessert
Malpua 64

For vegetarian

Starter
Cauliflower Kabab 78
Main Course
Lotus stems in an Exotic Curry 80
Stir-fried Mushrooms 86
Accompaniments
Daal Panchmela 44
Stuffed Parantha 36
Dahi Bhalla 92
Dessert
Besan Ladoo 68

Picnic

Starter
Chicken Tikka 24
Assorted Fritters 98
Main Course
Pomegranate Potatoes 100
Ginger Lamb Chops 38
Accompaniments
Poori 24
Lemon Rice 12
Tomato Chutney 100
Dessert
Besan Ladoo 68

Starter
Lamb Seekh Kebab 44
Main Course
Chicken Black Pepper 20
Crunchy Okra 92
Accompaniments
Daal Makhani 40
Mushroom Pulao 20
Khameeri Roti 28
Dessert
Malpua 64

Starters
Prawn Cutlets 60
Barbecued Chicken Drumsticks 22
Cottage Cheese Croquettes 82

Main Course
Potatoes in Chutney 88
Accompaniments
Daal Makhani 40
Mint Chutney 102
Naan 34
Dessert
Coconut Burfee 72

Starters
Fish Tikka 62
Batter coated Stuffed Tomatoes 94
Main Course
Minced Lamb with Peas 36
Accompaniments
Jackfruit Pulao 18
Dahi Bhalla 92
Mint Chutney 102

Dessert
Imarti 62

Starters
Sesame Prawn Tikka 58
Tandoori Chicken Chaat 42
Main Course
Mushrooms in Tomato Gravy 88
Stir-Fried Lamb Delight 46
Accompaniments
Mushroom Pulao 20
Lachha Parantha 32
Mint Chutney 102
Dessert
Lavang Latika 60

For vegetarian

Starters
Yoghurt flavoured, Cottage Cheese cutlets 100
Steamed Savory Gramflour Dish 72
Batter coated stuffed Tomatoes 94
Accompaniments
Stuffed Parantha 36
Broccoli and Carrot Pulao 8
Boondi Raita 96
Dessert
Gajrela 74

CHICKEN IN A FLAVOURED GRAVY

Serves: 4

Preparation time: 20 minutes

Cooking time: 30 minutes

Chicken with Spinach

Ingredients

Chicken, skinned and cut into pieces 1 kg
Oil 60 ml / 4 tbs
Cinnamon sticks 4
Bayleaves *(tej patta)* 2
Ginger paste (page 105) 45 gms / 3 tbs
Garlic paste (page 105) 45 gms / 3 tbs
Onion paste (page 105) 200 gms / 1 cup
Red chilli powder 10 gms / 2 tsp
Tomatoes, chopped 180 gms / ¾ cup
Spinach *(palak)*, puréed
350 gms / 1¾ cups
Maize flour *(makke ka atta)*
3 gms / ½ tsp
Water 45 ml / 3 tbs
Butter 100 gms / ½ cup
Salt to taste
White pepper powder 3 gms / ½ tsp
Ginger juliennes 10 gms / 2 tsp
Fenugreek powder *(methi)* 3 gms / ⅔ tsp

Method

1 Heat the oil in a pan, add cinnamon and bay leaves and sauté over medium heat until they begin to crackle.

2 Add the ginger, garlic and onion pastes and red chilli powder, and sauté for 30-60 seconds.

3 Add tomatoes and sauté further for 1 minute.

4 Add the spinach purée, stir in maize flour diluted with water and cook over medium heat for 10-15 minutes, stirring occasionally.

5 In another pan heat the butter and sauté the chicken until lightly browned.

6 Transfer the chicken pieces into the spinach sauce. Add salt and white pepper powder, cover and simmer on very low heat (dum) for 10-15 minutes or till chicken is cooked.

7 Serve garnished with ginger juliennes and fenugreek powder.

CHICKEN WITH SPINACH

Serves: 4-5

Preparation time: 10 minutes

Cooking time: 45 minutes

Tomato Flavoured Chicken

Ingredients

Chicken (cut into 12 pieces) 1 kg
Garam masala (page 105) 5 gms / 1 tsp
Garlic paste (page 105) 20 gms / 4 tsp
Ginger, chopped 45 gms / 3 tbs
Green chillies, sliced 2
Oil 100 ml / ½ cup
Red and Green Bell peppers
115 gms / 1 cup
Red chilli, pounded coarsely 6-8
Tomatoes, blanched and chopped 1 kg
Green coriander, chopped 5 gms / 1 tsp

Method

1 Heat oil in a *kadhai* (wok), sauté garlic paste, add red chillies, fry a while, add chopped tomatoes and cook for 5 minutes, stirring constantly.

2 Add ginger, sliced green chillies and salt, cook on medium heat for 3-5 minutes.

3 Add chicken pieces and cook till the gravy is thick and the chicken is tender.

4 Stir in red and green peppers, garam masala. Cover and cook for 3-4 minutes.

5 Garnish with chopped coriander and serve hot, accompanied by Naan (page 34).

TOMATO FLAVOURED CHICKEN

Serves: 4

Preparation time: 30 minutes

Cooking time: 30 minutes

EXOTIC CHICKEN DUMPLINGS

Ingredients

For the dumplings:
Chicken, minced 1 kg
Cumin *(jeera)* powder 3 gms / ½ tsp
Black cumin *(shah jeera)* powder a pinch
Black cardamom *(bari elaichi)* powder 3 gms / ½ tsp
Cinnamon *(daalchini)* powder a pinch
Black cardamom *(bari elaichi)* 3
Asafoetida *(heeng)* small pinch
Red chilli powder 5 gms / 1 tsp
Mustard oil 40 ml / 2 ⅔ tbs
Fennel *(saunf)* powder 5 gms / 1 tsp

For the stuffing:
Dried plums *(aloo bukhara)* 100 gms

For the curry:
Mustard oil 100 ml / ½ cup
Cloves *(laung)* 4
Red chilli powder 15 gms / 1 tbs
Water 1½ ltr / 7 cups
Green cardamoms *(choti elaichi)* 4
Black cardamoms *(bari elaichi)* 4
Bay leaves *(tej patta)* 2
Black cumin *(shah jeera)* 2 gms / ⅓ tsp
Salt to taste
Turmeric *(haldi)* powder 10 gms / 2 tsp
Black cardamom *(bari elaichi)* powder 10 gms / 2 tsp
Fennel *(saunf)* powder 15 gms / 1 tbs
Cinnamon *(daalchini)* powder 6 gms / 1 tsp
Tomatoes, chopped 200 gms / 1 cup

Method

1 **For the dumplings,** combine all the ingredients, mix well and divide into 16 equal portions.

2 Place one dried plum in the centre of each portion. Shape into balls and keep aside.

3 **For the curry,** heat oil in *kadhai* (wok) till it is smoking. Add the cloves, when they begin to crackle, reduce the flame.

4 Add red chilli powder, wait for oil to turn red, add water and bring to a boil.

5 Mix in the remaining whole spices and powdered spices. Bring to a boil and add the chicken dumplings gently.

6 Cook for 25-30 minutes, till the curry thickens and the dumplings are fully cooked.

7 Remove into a serving dish and serve hot, accompanied by any Indian bread.

Exotic Chicken Dumplings

Serves: 4

Preparation time: 25 minutes

Cooking time: 1 hour 30 minutes

Chicken Almond Steaks

Ingredients

Chicken, escalopes 600 gms
Egg, whisked 1
Salt 12 gms / 2 tsp
Red chilli powder 7 gms / 1 ½ tsp
Lemon juice 10 gms / 2 tsp
Ginger-garlic paste (pg. 105) 25 gms / 5 tsp
Oil for frying 10 gms / 2 tsp
Almonds, blanched 75 gms / 5 tbs
Yoghurt 100 gms / ½ cup
Butter 30 gms / 2 tbs
Ginger-garlic paste (pg. 105) 15 gms / 1 tbs
White pepper powder 3 gms / ½ tsp
Brown onion paste 30 gms / 2 tbs
Tomato purée 75 gms / 5 tbs
Cream 45 gms / 3 tbs
Garam masala (pg. 105) a pinch
Cream 5 gms / 1 tsp
Almonds, slivered 10 gms / 2 tsp

Method

1 **For the batter,** mix together, egg, salt (1 tsp), red chilli powder (½ tsp), lemon juice and ginger-garlic paste (5 tsp). Flatten out each escalope with a steak hammer and coat with the prepared batter. Refrigerate for 15 minutes.

2 Heat oil in a pan and shallow fry the chicken pieces until golden brown on both sides. Remove from heat, drain excess oil and keep aside.

3 **For the gravy,** grind the almonds to a fine past and blend with yoghurt.

4 Heat oil and butter in a pan, add ginger-garlic paste and sauté for a few seconds. Add yoghurt and sauté, stir in the remaining salt and red chilli powder alongwith white pepper powder and cook for a few seconds.

5 Stir in onion paste, tomato purée, cream and sauté for 8-10 minutes. Add chicken pieces to the gravy and cook on low heat till the pieces are tender and the curry reduces to half.

6 Remove the chicken pieces from the gravy and place on a serving platter, pour the gravy on top. Sprinkle garam masala and drizzle cream. Serve hot, garnished with slivered almonds.

CHICKEN ALMOND STEAKS

Serves: 4

Preparation time: 15 minutes

Cooking time: 40 minutes

Pomegranate Chicken

Ingredients

Chicken, cut into boneless pieces 700 gms
Ginger-garlic paste (pg. 105) 15 gms / 1 tbs
Salt 8 gms / 1½ tsp
Red chilli powder 4 gms / ¾ tsp
Oil 40 ml / 2 ⅔ tbs
Cashewnut paste 60 gms / 4 tbs
Yoghurt 50 gms / 3 ⅓ tbs
Water 200 ml / 1 cup
Brown onion paste (pg. 105) 20 gms / 4 tsp
Tomato purée (pg. 105) 45 gms / 3 tbs
Pomegranate (anardana) seeds 100 gms / ½ cups
Cream 45 gms / 3 tbs
Garam masala (pg. 105) 3 gms / ½ tsp

Method

1 Wash, clean and dry the chicken pieces. Marinate the chicken pieces with ginger-garlic paste (2 tsp), half of salt and red chilli powder and keep aside for 10-15 minutes.

2 Heat oil (30 ml) in a pan. Sauté the chicken pieces for a few minutes without letting the colour change. Keep aside.

3 Add the remaining oil to the pan, sauté the remaining ginger-garlic paste for 2-3 minutes. Add cashewnut paste mixed with yoghurt and water. Season with remaining salt and red chilli powder, simmer for 8-10 minutes.

4 Add the brown onion paste, tomato purée and chicken pieces and cook on low heat till the chicken is tender and the curry has thickened.

5 Extract juice from pomegranate seeds and strain through a muslin cloth into the simmering curry.

6 Stir in the cream. Remove from heat, transfer to a serving dish, and serve hot, garnished with garam masala.

POMEGRANATE CHICKEN

Serves: 4

Preparation time: 20 minutes

Cooking time: 25 minutes

Chicken with Black Pepper

Ingredients

Chicken drumstick 800 gms
Ginger paste (pg. 105) 10 gms / 2 tsp
Garlic paste (pg. 105) 10 gms / 2 tsp
Turmeric *(haldi)* powder 2 gms / ½ tsp
Red chilli paste 10 gms / 2 tsp
Salt to taste
Oil for frying
Black peppercorn, crushed 10 gms / 2 tsp
Lemon juice 45 ml / 3 tbs
Salt to taste
Green coriander, chopped 20 gms / 4 tsp
Garam masala (pg. 105) 3 gms / ½ tsp

Method

1 **For the marinade,** mix together the ginger and garlic pastes, turmeric, red chilli paste and salt.

2 Marinate the chicken drumsticks in this mixture and keep aside for 2 hours.

3 Heat oil in a pan and fry chicken till golden brown in colour, remove and keep aside.

4 In a *kadhai* (wok), add chicken alongwith marinade and all other ingredients, stir-fry till chicken is fully cooked. Serve hot, accompanied by any Indian bread.

CHICKEN WITH BLACK PEPPER

Serves: 4

Preparation time: 2 hours

Cooking time: 40 minutes

Chicken in a Rich Creamy Gravy

Ingredients

Tandoori chicken
(cut into 8 pieces each) 2
Bay leaf 1
Butter 120 gms / 2/3 cup
Cinnamon sticks 2
Cream 150 ml / ¾ cup
Garlic paste (pg. 105) 45 gms / 3 tbs
Ginger julienned 10 gms / 2 tsp
Ginger paste 45 gms / 3 tbs
Green cardamoms *(choti elaichi)* 10
Green chillies (slit and deseeded) 5
Green coriander, chopped 15 gms / 1 tbs
Honey 15 ml / 1 tbs
Paprika or Red chilli powder 5 gms / 1 tsp
Salt to taste
Tomatoes, chopped 900 gms / 4 ½ cups
Water 200 ml / 1 cup

Method

1 Melt half the butter in a thick bottom pan, sauté for 30 seconds the cinnamon, cardamoms and bay leaf, stir in the ginger and garlic pastes, and cook till the water evaporates.

2 Add tomatoes and salt and cook till the tomatoes dissolve. Add 2 cups of water and let it simmer for some time.

3 Strain the gravy through a soup strainer into another pan.

4 Melt the remaining butter in a kadhai/wok, add the ginger juliennes and green chillies and sauté for a minute. Add the paprika—the colour of the mixture will turn a bright red. Add the strained gravy and bring to a boil.

5 Add the tandoori chicken pieces and simmer for 10 minutes till the chicken gets soft. Stir in the cream and honey.

6 Serve, garnished with green coriander and accompanied by any Indian bread.

Chicken in a Rich Creamy Gravy

Serves: 4-5

Preparation time: 20 minutes + time to roast the chicken, if tandoori chicken is not available

Cooking time: 25 minutes

Stir-fried Chicken with Spring Onions

Ingredients

Chicken, cut into boneles cubes 800 gms
Onion, chopped 200 gms / 1 cup
Tomato, finely chopped 100 gms / ½ cup
Mustard oil 75 ml / 5 tbs
Mustard *(raee)* seeds 10 gms / 2 tsp
Red chilli powder to taste
Salt to taste
Cumin *(jeera)* powder 10 gms / 2 tsp
Ginger-Garlic paste (pg. 105)
45 gms / 3 tbs
Spring onion, leaves 100 gms / ½ cup

Method

1 Heat oil (2 tbs) in a kadhai (wok), sauté onion till transparent. Add tomatoes and cook for 10-15 minutes. Keep aside.

2 In a separate *kadhai* (wok), heat the remaining oil, add mustard seeds and sauté till they crackle.

3 Stir in the onion-tomato mixture, cook for 3-4 minutes. Add the the chicken, salt and red chilli powder.

4 Cook further for 20 minutes on low heat, till the chicken is done.

5 Mix in the spring onion, cook for 2 minutes.

6 Remove from heat and serve hot, accompanied by any Indian bread.

STIR-FRIED CHICKEN WITH SPRING ONIONS

Serves: 4

Preparation time: 15 minutes

Cooking time: 1 hour

Stir Fried Chicken

Ingredients

Chicken 1.2 kg
Red chilli powder 3 gms / ½ tsp
Turmeric *(haldi)* powder 5 gms/1 tsp
Salt to taste
Ginger paste (pg. 105) 45 gms / 3 tbs
Garlic paste (pg. 105) 30 gms / 6 tsp
Groundnut oil 80 ml / 1/3 cup
Tamarind *(imlee)* 25 gms / 5 tsp
Onions, chopped 75 gms / 5 tbs
Curry leaves 12
Tomatoes, chopped 120 gms / ½ cup
Green cardamom *(choti elaichi)* powder 3 gm / ½ tsp
Coriander leaves, chopped 20 gms / 4 tsp
Clove *(laung)* powder 3 gms / ½ tsp
Cinnamon *(daalchini)* powder 3 gms / ½ tsp
Black peppercorns, pounded 3 gms / ½ tsp
Coriander powder 3 gms / ½ tsp
Lemon juice 15 ml / 3 tbs

Method

1 Clean the chicken, debone and cut into 1½ inch cubes.

2 Mix red chillies, turmeric and salt with half of the ginger and garlic pastes and rub this marinade onto the chicken pieces. Keep aside for 30 minutes.

3 Heat oil in a kadhai, add the marinaded chicken and sauté over medium heat until evenly light brown. Remove and reserve oil.

4 Soak the tamarind in (5 tsp) water for 10 minutes, mash well, squeeze out pulp and discard.

5 Reheat reserved oil, add the curry leaves and stir. Add onions and sauté until light brown. Add remaining ginger-garlic paste, and tomatoes. Cook till oil seperates.

6 Stir in cardamom, coriander, clove and cinnamon powder alongwith taramind. Cook for 5 minutes. Add chicken pieces and water (1 cup), bring to a boil and cook till the gravy coats the chicken pieces.

7 Sprinkle black peppercorns and lemon juice. Serve hot.

Stir Fried Chicken

Serves: 4

Preparation time: 1 hour

Cooking time: 45 minutes

TANDOORI CHICKEN

Ingredients

Chicken broiler, skinless
(600 gms each) 2
Salt to taste
Red chilli paste 25 gms / 5 tsp
Ginger paste (pg. 105) 10 gms / 2 tsp
Garlic paste (pg. 105) 45 gms / 3 tbs
Lemon juice 30 ml / 2 tbs
Butter, for basting 50 gms / ¼ cup
Chaat masala 5 gms / 1 tsp
Cream 10 ml / 2 tsp

For the marinade:

Cumin powder *(jeera)* 5 gms / 1 tsp
Garam masala (pg. 105) 10 gms / 2 tsp
Ginger paste (pg. 105) 25 gms / 5 tsp
Lemon juice 30 ml / 2 tbs
Oil 60 ml / 4 tbs
Red chilli paste 25 gms / 5 tsp
Saffron a few strands
Salt to taste
Yoghurt, drained 200 gms / 1 cup

Method

1 Make incisions—3 each on breasts and thighs and 2 each on drumsticks.

2 Mix the salt, red chilli paste, ginger and garlic pastes and lemon juice, rub this paste into the chicken. Keep aside for 30 minutes.

3 Whisk yoghurt in a large bowl and mix all the ingredients for the marinade.

4 Coat the chicken with the marinade and leave in the refrigerator for 5-6 hours.

5 Preheat the oven or tandoor to 175 °C (350 °F).

6 Skewer the chickens from head to tail, leaving a 4 cm gap between each. Keep a tray underneath to collect excess drippings.

7 Roast approximately for 15 minutes or until almost done. Remove and baste with butter, then roast for another 5 minutes.

8 Remove the chicken from the skewer, cut each into four pieces and arrange on a platter. Sprinkle chaat masala and cream and serve hot.

Tandoori Chicken

Serves: 4

Preparation time: 6 hours

Cooking time: 25 minutes

Slow Oven Tandoori Chicken

Ingredients

For the parda dough:

Butter 50 gms / ¼ cup
Cream 120 ml / ½ cup
Egg yolks 2
Flour 150 gms / ¾ cup
Milk 100 ml / ½ cup
Salt to taste
Sugar 10 gms / 2 tsp
Vetivier *(kewda)* 2 drops

Method

1 **Follow the master recipe for tandoori chicken (pg. 28) till the chicken is half cooked—approximately 5 minutes.**

2 Sieve the flour with the salt into a mixing bowl.

3 Dissolve the sugar in warm milk, add the vetivier and stir.

4 Pour the milk mixture into the flour, knead into a dough and keep aside for 15 minutes.

5 Add melted butter to the dough, knead the dough again and keep aside for 10 minutes.

6 Divide dough into 2 equal portions, make a ball and dust with flour. Leave aside for another 5 minutes.

7 Grease 2 casserole dishes, one for each chicken.

8 Roll out the dough into discs, the size of each casserole dish. Prick the surface of the dough with a fork.

9 Preheat the oven to 150 °C (300 °F).

10 Cut the chicken into four pieces and arrange in the casserole. Sprinkle half the cream on the chicken and cover with the dough *(parda)*. Brush with beaten egg yolk.

11 Repeat this process with the second chicken and dough.

12 Bake for 10-15 minutes, until the pastry *(parda)* is golden brown.

13 Cut open the parda and serve the chicken along with a portion of the parda.

Slow Oven Tandoori Chicken

Serves: 4-5

Preparation time: 40 minutes + 6 hours for tandoori chicken

Cooking time: 20 minutes

Slow oven Chicken with a hint of Fenugreek

Ingredients

Chicken 1 kg / 2 small birds, cut into 6 pieces each
Green cardamoms *(choti elaichi)* 5
Cinnamon 1" stick, Cloves *(laung)* 8
Green coriander, chopped 15 gms / 1 tbs
Dough to seal casserole
Fenugreek *(methi)*, dry leaves 15 gms / 1 tbs
or fresh leaves 60 gms / ¼ cup
Garlic, chopped 30 gms / 2 tbs
Ginger, chopped 30 gms / 2 tbs
Ginger julienned 20 gms / 4 tsp
Green chillies, slit 5
Oil 75 gms / 5 tbs
Onions, chopped 360 gms / 1½ cups
Red chilli powder 5 gms / 1 tsp
Salt to taste
Tomatoes, chopped 240 gms / 1 cup
Yoghurt 240 gms / 1 cup

Method

1 Marinade chicken in whisked yoghurt and salt for half an hour.

2 Meanwhile, heat fat in a kadhai, crackle cardamoms, cloves and cinnamon. Add onions and sauté till golden brown. Stir in chopped garlic, ginger and green chillies. Add red chilli powder and tomatoes and stir-cook till fat surfaces.

3 Add chicken with the marinade and 240 ml/1 cup water. Bring to boil, cover and simmer till the fat is visible on the sides once again and the chicken is tender.

4 Remove to an oven proof casserole, sprinkle with fenugreek, ginger juliennes and coriander, cover and seal with dough. Place in a preheated oven at 325 °F for 15 minutes.

5 Open casserole and serve simmering hot with any Indian bread

Slow oven Chicken with a hint of Fenugreek

Serves: 4

Preparation time: 45 minutes

Cooking time: 45 minutes

Tangy Chicken

Ingredients

Chicken breasts 12
Yoghurt 240 gms / 1 cup
Ginger paste (pg. 105) 20 gms / 4 tsp
Garlic paste (pg. 105) 20 gms / 4 tsp
Salt to taste
Black pepper powder 5 gms / 1 tsp
Lemon juice 30 ml / 2 tbs
Green chillies, chopped 4
Almond paste 45 gms / 3 tbs
Cumin *(jeera)* seeds 5 gms / 1 tsp
Onions, cut in rings 160 gms / 3/4 cup
Capsicum, cut in rings 100 gms
Saffron a pinch, dissolved in 1 tbs milk
White butter 60 gms / 4 tbs

Method

1 Hang yoghurt in a muslin cloth until reduced by half. Meanwhile, clean and debone chicken breasts.

2 Make a marinade of yoghurt, ginger and garlic pastes, salt, black pepper powder, lemon juice, green chillies and almond paste, cumin and marinade the chicken in it for half an hour.

3 Grease an oven proof shallow dish. Place the chicken pieces in it, without overlapping. Arrange the onion and capsicum rings over the chicken pieces and pour the left over marinade evenly over it.

4 Dot with dollops of remaining butter and roast in a preheated oven at 300 °F for 20 minutes.

5 Remove, sprinkle saffron, cover and let simmer in the oven for another 10 minutes.

6 Uncover dish, wipe edges and serve simmering hot, accompanied by Naan (page 34).

TANGY CHICKEN

Serve: 4

Preparation: 45 minutes

Cooking: 20 minutes

Minced Lamb with Peas

Ingredients

Lamb, minced 600 gms
Oil for frying
Onion, chopped 75 gms / 5 tbs
Tomatoes, chopped 75 gms / 5 tbs
Bayleaf *(tej patta)* 2
Peppercorns 3 gms / ½ tsp
Cloves *(laung)* 3 gms / ½ tsp
Black cardamoms *(bari elaichi)* 3 gms / ½ tsp
Green cardamoms *(choti elaichi)* 3 gms / ½ tsp
Coriander powder 10 gms / 2 tsp
Cumin *(jeera)* powder 10 gms / 2 tsp
Red chilli powder 5 gms / 1 tsp
Garam masala (pg. 105) 10 gms / 2 tsp
Green coriander, chopped 10 gms / 2 tsp
Salt to taste
Ginger, julienned 10 gms / 2 tsp
Ginger paste (pg. 105) 45 gms / 3 tbs
Garlic paste (pg. 105) 45 gms / 3 tbs
Green peas, boiled 100 gms / ½ cup

Method

1 Heat oil in a *kadhai* (wok), sauté onions till transparent, add tomatoes and cook for 10-15 minutes, remove from heat.

2 Heat oil in a separate *kadhai* (wok), add bayleaf, peppercorns, cloves and both cardamoms, sauté till they begin to crackle.

3 Pour in the onion-tomato mixture and then add minced lamb to it. Cook for 10-15 minutes.

4 Add the remaining ingredients and cook till oil seperates.

5 Add green peas and cook for another 10-15 minutes.

6 Remove from heat and serve hot, accompanied by Naan (page 34).

MINCED LAMB WITH PEAS

Serves: 4

Preparation time: 20 minutes

Cooking time: 40-50 minutes

Ginger Lamb Chops

Ingredients

Lamb chops 12
Papaya paste 30 gms / 2 tbs
Salt to taste
Ginger paste (pg. 105) 45 gms / 3 tbs
Garlic paste (pg. 105) 20 gms / 4 tsp
Black pepper powder 5 gms / 1 tsp
Cream 45 gms / 3 tbs
Cumin *(jeera)* powder 15 gms / 1 tbs
Red chilli powder 10 gms / 2 tsp
Garam masala (pg. 105) 10 gms / 2 tsp
Lemon juice 30 gms / 2 tbs
Butter/Oil for basting

Method

1 Clean chops and flatten them slightly with a spatula. Mix together, the papaya paste, salt, ginger-garlic pastes and pepper, rub it into the chops. Keep aside for 3-4 hours.

2 Whisk cream alongwith cumin powder, red chilli powder, garam masala and lemon juice. Coat the chops well and leave to marinate further for an hour.

3 Preheat oven to 175 °C (350 °F). Skewer chops an inch apart and roast in oven/tandoor/grill for 10-12 minutes.

4 Hang skewers for a couple of minutes to let excess liquids drip. Baste with butter and roast again for 3-4 minutes until lightly browned. Garnish with chopped coriander and serve hot.

Ginger Lamb Chops

Serves: 4

Preparation time: 4 hours 30 minutes

Cooking time: 20 minutes

Spicy Lamb Chops

Ingredients

Lamb chops, cleaned 16
Clarified butter *(ghee)* / Oil
200 gms /1 cup
Onions, chopped
500 gms / 2½ cups
Green cardamom *(choti elaichi)* 10
Cloves *(laung)* 4
Cinnammon *(daalchini)* sticks 4
Bayleaves *(tej patta)* 2
Ginger-garlic paste (pg. 105) 30 gms / 2 tbs
Tomatoes, chopped
700 gms / 3½ cups
Garam masala (pg. 105) 15 gms / 1 tbs
Coriander powder 15 gms / 1 tbs
Red chilli powder 15 gms / 1 tbs
Turmeric *(haldi)* powder 3 gms / ½ tsp
Salt to taste
Cashewnut paste 100 gms / ½ cup
Yoghurt 225 gms / 1 cup
Ginger, julienned 20 gms / 4 tsp
Green coriander, chopped
20 gms / 4 tsp

Method

1 Heat clarified butter/oil in a *kadhai* (wok), add onions and sauté over medium heat.

2 Add all the ingredients and mix well. Add cashewnut paste, stir-fry until the oil seperates. Stir in the yoghurt.

3 Add lamb chops, cover and cook, stirring occasionally until the lamb chops are tender and gravy thickens.

4 Serve hot, garnished with julienned ginger and chopped coriander.

SPICY LAMB CHOPS

Serves: 4

Preparation time: 30 minutes

Cooking time: 1 hour

Lamb Stir-cooked in a Spicy Gravy

Ingredients

Lamb (preferably chops) 1 kg
Salt to taste
Oil 60 ml / 4 tbs
Sugar 5 gms / 1 tsp
Cloves 10
Bayleaves *(tej patta)* 3
Green cardamoms 8
Cinnamon sticks 2
Onions, chopped 180 gms / ¾ cup
Red chilli powder 10 gms / 2 tsp
Black cumin seeds *(shah jeera)* 3 gms / ⅓ tsp
Tomatoes, skinned, deseeded and chopped 400 gms / 2 cups
Ginger paste (pg. 105) 10 gms / 2 tsp
Lamb stock / Water 200 ml / 1 cup
Fennel *(saunf)* powder 5 gms / 1 tsp

Method

1 Remove excess fat, pat with a paper towel, sprinkle with salt and keep aside for 10 minutes.

2 Heat oil, add sugar, cloves, bay leaves, green cardamoms and cinnamon sticks and sauté for 2-3 minutes.

3 Add the lamb chops and cook over medium heat until they are lightly browned.

4 Add the chopped onions and sauté till browned.

5 Add red chilli powder, black cumin seeds, chopped tomatoes and ginger paste, fry till oil separates from the gravy.

6 Add the stock/water and cook until the chops are tender. Stir in fennel seed powder. Cover and simmer for 10 minutes on a low fire.

7 Serve hot, garnished with a pinch of fennel seed powder, accompanied by steamed rice or Tandoori Roti (page 38).

LAMB STIR-COOKED IN A SPICY GRAVY

Serves: 4-5

Preparation time: 15 minutes

Cooking time: 35 minutes

Lamb Cooked in Whole Spices

Ingredients

Lamb, cut into boneless cubes 900 gms
Oil 125 ml / 3/4 cup
Cinnamon *(daalchini)* sticks 2
Cloves *(laung)* 5
Nutmeg *(jaiphal)* 1
Green cardamom *(choti elaichi)* 4
Ginger-garlic paste (pg. 105) 45 gms / 3 tbs
Onions, chopped 200 gms / 1 cup
Salt to taste
Red chilli powder 6 gms / 1 tsp
Garam masala (pg. 105) 5 gms / 1 tsp
Coriander powder 8 gms / 1½ tsp
Turmeric *(haldi)* powder 5 gms / 1 tsp
Tomato purée, fresh (pg. 105) 200 gms / 1 cup
Khoya, grated (pg. 105) 30 gms / 2 tbs
Yoghurt 45 gms / 3 tbs
Onion paste, browned (pg. 105) 45 gms / 3 tbs
Green peas, shelled 100 gms / ½ cup
Carrots, cut into rounds 200 gms / 1 cup
Mushroom, stems removed 80 gms / 1/3 cup
Cashewnuts, whole 150 gms / 2/3 cup
Water 800 ml / 4 cups

Method

1 Heat oil in a handi (pot), add the whole spices and sauté till they crackle, add ginger-garlic paste and sauté for 3-5 minutes.

2 Add the lamb cubes and onions. Cook on medium heat, until moisture dries out. Add salt and all the spices.

3 Stir in tomato purée and cook till it leaves oil.

4 Mix in all the remaining ingredients. Stir for a few seconds and add water.

5 Reduce heat and cook till the lamb pieces are tender and the gravy thickens. Remove from heat.

6 Transfer to a serving dish and serve hot, accompanied by Naan (page 34).

LAMB COOKED IN WHOLE SPICES

Serves: 4

Preparation Time: 20 minutes

Cooking Time: 1 hour

STIR-FRIED LAMB DELIGHT

Ingredients

Lamb (leg or shoulder) 1 kg
Almonds, blanched and cut into thin slivers 12
Coconut milk 250 gms / 1¼ cup
Fresh coriander, chopped 115 gms / 1 cup
Garlic, ground 20 gms / 4 tsp
Ginger, ground 25 gms / 5 tsp
Green chillies, whole 3
Oil 175 ml / 1 cup
Raisins, cut into halves 15 gms / 1 tbs
Red chillies, whole 3
Salt to taste
Yoghurt 400 gms / 2 cups

Method

1 Clean lamb and cut into pieces. Add ginger and garlic to the meat and marinade for 2 hours.

2 Heat oil, fry almonds and raisins separately to golden brown. Keep aside.

3 In the same oil, add the meat and fry till brown.

4 Mix in salt and yoghurt. Cook till the yoghurt dries up.

5 Stir in green and red chillies and chopped coriander.

6 Then add coconut milk and cook on low flame, stirring regularly without adding any water. When the lamb is tender, add almonds and raisins. Cover the pan and simmer till all the liquids have dried up.

7 Serve hot, accompanied by Naan (page 34).

STIR-FRIED LAMB DELIGHT

Serves: 4-6

Preparation time: 3 hours 30 minutes

Cooking time: 1 hour 30 minutes

Lamb Cooked in Rare Spices

Ingredients

Lamb, cut into pieces 1 kg
Oil 200 ml / 1 cup
Green cardamom *(choti elaichi)* 10
Black cardamom *(bari elaichi)* 2
Cinnamon *(daalchini)* sticks 2
Cloves *(laung)* 5
Nutmeg *(jaiphal)* 1
Ginger-garlic paste (pg. 105) 20 gms / 4 tsp
Red chilli powder 5 gms / 1 tsp
Turmeric *(haldi)* powder 5 gms / 1 tsp
Salt 10 gm / 2 tsp
Onion paste (pg. 105) 200 gms / 1 cup
Brown onion paste (pg. 105) 45 gms / 3 tbs

For the curry:

Nihari Masala, Har /Baheda/Amla *(trifla)*, Dry ginger powder *(sonth)*, Fennel *(saunf)* seeds, Cumin *(jeera)* seeds, Coconut 5 gms /1 tsp
Garam masala (pg. 105) 5 gms / 1 tsp
Tomato purée, fresh (pg. 105) 150 gms / 3/4 cup
Water 600 ml / 3 cup
Khoya, grated (pg. 105) 15 gms / 1 tbs
Chickpea powder, roasted 75 gms / 5 tbs
Saffron *(kesar)* a few strands

Method

1 Wash, clean and dry the lamb pieces.

2 Heat oil in a pan, add green cardamom, black cardomon, cinnamon, cloves and nutmeg. When they crackle, stir in the ginger-garlic paste, red chilli powder, turmeric powder and salt, stir fry for 4-5 minutes.

3 Add onion paste and cook on low heat stirring constantly. Sprinkle a little water as and when required. Cover and cook for 15-20 minutes.

4 Stir in the brown onion paste, nihari masala and garam masala, stir-fry till the oil seperates.

5 Add water, khoya and chickpea powder.

6 Add the lamb pieces along with saffron, cover and cook on very low heat for 25-30 minutes or till the lamb pieces are tender and the gravy thickens.

7 Remove from heat, transfer to a serving bowl and serve hot.

LAMB COOKED IN RARE SPICES

Serves: 4

Preparation time: 30 minutes

Cooking time: 1 hour

Pickled Lamb Curry

Ingredients

Lamb chops 8 pieces
Raw papaya, a small piece pounded
Ginger paste (pg. 105) 10 gms / 2 tsp
Garlic paste (pg. 105) 10 gms / 2 tsp
Salt to taste
Gramflour *(besan)* 10 gms / 2 tsp
Aniseed 5 gms / 1 tsp
Black cardamoms 3 gms / ½ tsp
Black pepper 5 gms / 1 tsp
Cloves 3 gms / ½ tsp
Meat tenderizer 5 gms/ 1 tsp
Mustard oil *(sarson ka tel)* 50 ml / 3⅓ tbs
Chaat masala 5 gms / 1 tsp
Mustard *(raee)* seeds 5 gms / 1 tsp
Onion *(kalonji)* seeds 5 gms / 1 tsp
Lemon juice 15 ml / 1 tbs
Red chilli powder 15 gms / 1 tbs
Yoghurt, whisked 50 gms / ¼ cup

Method

1 Flatten the chops with a steak hammer. Rub with papaya, ginger and garlic pastes, salt and keep aside.

2 Heat the gramflour in a pan till light brown and sprinkle over the lamb chops.

3 Add the remaining ingredients (except chaat masala and lemon juice) to the yoghurt and mix well. Marinate the chops in this mixture for 2 hours.

4 Preheat the oven to 175 °C (350 °F).

5 Skewer the chops and roast in a hot tandoor or oven until cooked, basting occasionally.

6 Remove the chops from the skewer. Sprinkle chaat masala and lemon juice and serve hot.

PICKLED LAMB CURRY

Serves: 4-5

Preparation time: 2 hours 30 minutes

Cooking time: 30 minutes

Lamb Curry

Ingredients

Lamb (cut into boneless cubes) 1 kg
Almond paste 50 gms / ¼ cup
Bay leaves *(tej patta)* 2
Butter (unsalted) 100 gms / ½ cup
Cinnamon sticks 5
Clarified butter *(ghee)* 150 gms / ¾ cup
Cream 100 ml / ½ cup
Garlic paste (pg. 105) 25 gms / 5 tsp
Ginger paste (pg. 105) 25 gms / 5 tsp
Green cardamoms *(choti elaichi)* 10
Green cardamom *(choti elaichi)* powder 3 gms / ½ tsp
Green chillies 50 gms / 6-10
Onions, sliced 150 gms / ¾ cup
Salt to taste
White pepper powder 2 gms / ½ tsp
Yoghurt 250 gms / 1¼ cup

Method

1 Rub the ginger and garlic pastes over the lamb and keep aside for 1 hour.

2 Heat the clarified butter and butter. Fry bay leaves, cinnamon sticks and cardamoms till they crackle, then add onions and sauté till soft.

3 Add the cubed lamb and cook over high heat until the lamb changes colour.

4 Add yoghurt and almond paste and cook on low heat for another 25 minutes or until tender. Season to taste with cream, green chillies, white pepper powder, salt and green cardamom powder.

5 Serve hot, accompanied by Tandoori Roti (page 38).

LAMB CURRY

Serves: 4-5

Preparation time: 1 hour

Cooking time: 30 minutes

LAMB SHANKS IN GRAVY

Ingredients

Lamb meat from the shanks, on the bone, 1 kg / 10 pieces
Bayleaves *(tej patta)* 2
Black pepper powder 5 gms / 1 tsp
Cinnamon *(daalchini)* sticks 2
Cloves *(laung)* 8
Cumin *(jeera)* powder 3 gms / ½ tsp
Garlic paste (pg. 105) 45 gms / 3 tbs
Clarified butter *(ghee)* 60 ml / 4 tbs
Ginger, julienned 10 gms / 2 tsp
Ginger paste (pg. 105) 45 gms / 3 tbs
Green cardamoms *(choti elaichi)* 8
Green cardamom powder 3 gm / ½ tsp
Green coriander, chopped 5 gms / 1 tsp
Kashmiri red chilli powder 5 gms / 1 tsp
Mace powder *(javitri)* 5 gms / 1 tsp
Milk 15 ml / 1 tbs
Onions 175 gms / ¾ cup
Saffron 5 gms / 1 tsp
Salt to taste
Vetivier *(kewda)* 2 drops
Yoghurt 400 gms / 2 cups

Method

1 Heat clarified butter (1 tbs) in a pan and fry the onions. Grind to a paste and keep aside.

2 In the same pan, heat remaining clarified butter, add lamb shanks alongwith whole spices, ginger and garlic paste and salt. Cover and cook on low heat for 30 minutes, stirring occasionally.

3 Add yoghurt and stir-fry till liquids evaporate.

4 Add red chilli powder and onion paste dissolved in 5 tbs water.

5 Stir in half of black pepper powder, cumin powder and water (6 cups). Bring to a boil, reduce heat, cover and seal dough. Cook on low heat (dum) for 1 hour.

6 Unseal and remove lamb pieces into a bowl from the gravy. Strain the gravy and return to heat. Add mace, cardamom powder and saffron-vetivier mixed in milk.

7 Cook till gravy thickens. Pour over the lamb pieces and serve, garnished with julienned ginger and chopped coriander.

LAMB SHANKS IN GRAVY

Serves: 4-5

Preparation time: 15 minutes

Cooking time: 3 hours

Spicy Lamb Leg

Ingredients

Leg of lamb 1 kg
Mace *(javitri)* 10 gms / 2 tsp
Nutmeg *(jaiphal)* 1
Cloves 4
Aniseed 10 gms / 2 tsp
Cinnamon *(daalchini)* sticks 3
Black cardamoms *(bari elaichi)* 3
Green cardamoms *(choti elaichi)* 6
Onion, medium 1
Ginger 45 gms / 3 tbs
Red chilli powder 10 gms / 2 tsp
Salt to taste
Poppy seeds, soaked 10 gms / 2 tsp
Asafoetida *(heeng)*, crushed 3 gms / ½ tsp
Coconut, desiccated 10 gms / 2 tsp
Oil 200 ml / 1 cup
Yoghurt 45 gms / 3 tbs
Bay leaves *(tej patta)* 4
Fresh mint 10 gms / 2 tsp
Almonds, blanched 4
Green coriander, chopped 10 gms / 2 tsp

Method

1 Remove all the white membrane from the surface of the lamb. Prick repeatedly and thoroughly down to the bone, with a strong and large-pronged fork, until all the fibres are broken and the meat well-loosened. The success of this dish depends upon doing this well.

2 Grind together mace, nutmeg, cloves, cinnamon, black and green cardamoms, ginger, onion, salt, red chilli powder, salt, poppy seeds and coconut. Apply the ground spices evenly all over the leg and prick again so that the spices soak into the body of the meat. Marinate for 2 hours.

3 Tie the raan with a string so that the meat stays on the bone whilst cooking. Place the leg in a large pan.

4 Cover with a mixture of oil, yoghurt, bay leaves and aniseed. Add 1 litre of water, cover and cook on moderate heat until water is reduced to 150 ml.

5 Add the crushed asafoetida in 3 tsp of water, add this to the raan and cook until 100 ml of gravy is left.

6 Serve hot garnished with mint, almonds and green coriander.

Spicy Lamb Leg

Serves: 4-5

Preparation time: 2 hours 30 minutes

Cooking time: 3 hours 30 minutes

Fenugreek Flavoured Prawns

Ingredients

Prawns, shelled, deveined 1400 gms
Vinegar 45 ml / 3 tbs
Salt to taste
Lemon juice 20 ml / 4 tsp
Yoghurt 240 gms / 1 1/3 cup
Cream 200 gms / 1 cup
White pepper powder
8 gms / 1 ½ tsp
Cheese, grated 75 gms / 5 tbs
Dry fenugreek *(kasoori methi)* powder
5 gms / 1 tsp
Ginger-garlic paste (pg. 105) 45 gms / 3 tbs
Garam masala (pg. 105) 8 gms / 1 ½ tsp
Saffron *(kesar)* a few strands
Butter for basting

Method

1 Wash the prawns with vinegar and salt water. Drain and pat dry.

2 Prepare a marinade by mixing together all the ingredients except butter.

3 Marinate the prawns in the prepared marinade and keep aside for 30 minutes.

4 Skewer the prawns and roast in a moderately hot tandoor for 6-8 minutes. Remove from tandoor and allow excess liquids to drip.

5 Baste lightly with butter and roast again for 2-3 minutes.

6 Remove from skewers and serve, accompanied by Mint Chutney (page 102).

FENUGREEK FLAVOURED PRAWNS

Serves: 4

Preparation time: 40 minutes

Cooking time: 10 minutes

Shrimps in Coconut

Ingredients

Shrimps, peeled 600 gms
Oil 80 ml / 5 1/3 tbs
Mustard *(raee)* seeds 3 gms / ½ tsp
Curry leaves 2
Garlic, slivered 10 gms / 2 tsp
Onions, chopped 4
Green chilli, chopped 1
Coriander powder 6 gms / 1 tsp
Red chilli powder 5 gms / 1 tsp
Turmeric *(haldi)* powder 3 gms / ½ tsp
Coconut (fresh), grated 1
Cumin *(jeera)*, whole 10 gms / 2 tsp
Salt to taste
Coconut milk 200 ml / 1 cup

Method

1 Heat oil in a *kadhai* (wok), sauté mustard seeds till they crackle, add curry leaves, garlic slivers and chopped onions. Stir-fry till onions are transparent.

2 Stir in all other ingredients except for coconut milk. Cook till the oil separates and appears on the surface. Add water as and when necessary to cook the curry.

3 Add coconut milk alongwith shrimps, stir-fry till shrimps are cooked and curry thickens. Remove from heat.

4 Serve hot, accompanied by Tandoori Roti (page 38).

SHRIMPS IN COCONUT

Serves: 3-4

Preparation time: 25 minutes

Cooking time: 40-50 minutes

Fennel flavoured Prawns

Ingredients

Prawns, deveined and shelled 12
Fennel *(saunf)* seeds
broiled and pounded 10 gms / 2 tsp
Garlic, chopped 10 gms / 2 tsp
Green chillies, deseeded, chopped 5
Onion paste (pg. 105) 30 gms / 2 tbs
Lemon juice 30 ml / 2 tbs
Salt to taste
Fennel *(saunf)*, chopped 25 gms / 5 tsp
Cream 100 ml / ½ cup
Yoghurt 100 ml / ½ cup
Ginger, chopped 5 gms / 1 tsp
Butter 20 gms / 4 tsp

Method

1 Heat butter in a pan and sauté the chopped fennel for a few seconds.

2 Add garlic, green chillies and onion paste. Stir-fry for a few minutes.

3 Mix in all the other ingredients and cook for 5-10 minutes. Remove from heat.

4 Place prawns in an oven proof dish, pour the prepared mixture on top. Cover the dish tightly and cook in a preheated 175 °C (350 °F) oven for 15-20 minutes.

5 Remove from the oven. Transfer into a serving platter and serve immediately accompanied by steamed rice and Boondi Raita (page 96).

FENNEL FLAVOURED PRAWNS

Serves: 4

Preparation time: 25 minutes

Cooking time: 35-40 minutes

Tandoori Prawns

Ingredients

Prawns (king size) 12
Lemon juice 75 ml / 5 tbs
Ginger paste (pg. 105) 45 gms / 3 tbs
Garlic paste (pg. 105) 45 gms / 3 tbs
Salt to taste
Carom *(ajwain)* seeds 5 gms / 1 tsp
Yoghurt 480 ml / 2 1/3 cups
Yellow chilli powder 5 gms / 1 tsp
Chick-pea flour 45 gms / 3 tbs
Garam masala (pg. 105) 5 gms / 1 tsp
Turmeric *(haldi)* powder 3 gms / ½ tsp
Butter for basting
Chaat masala 5 gms / 1 tsp

Mcthod

1 Reserve 2 tablespoons lemon juice and mix the rest with the ginger and garlic pastes.

2 Add salt, chick-pea flour, carom seeds, yoghurt, yellow chilli powder, garam masala and turmeric powder. Marinade the prawns in this for 2 hours.

3 Arrange on skewers and cook in a tandoor till half done, about 5-7 minutes.

4 Remove and set aside for 10 minutes. Cook again in the tandoor for 2 minutes.

5 Baste with butter and replace in the tandoor for approximately 3 more minutes.

6 Remove from skewers and arrange on a platter. Sprinkle with chaat masala and the reserved lemon juice.

7 Serve hot, accompanied by a green salad.

Tandoori Prawns

Serves: 4

Preparation time: 2 hours

Cooking time: 15 minutes

Prawn Curry

Ingredients

Prawns, cleaned and deveined 1 kg
Beef or Chicken stock 150 ml / ¾ cup
Cinnamon *(daalchini)*, ground 5 gms /1 tsp
Cloves *(laung)*, ground 5 gms / 1 tsp
Creamed coconut 100 gms / ½ cup
Flour 5 gms / 1 tsp
Garlic, crushed 5 gms / 1 tsp
Lemon juice 5 gms / 1 tsp
Oil 100 ml / ½ cup
Onion, finely chopped 1
Red chilli powder 10 gms / 2 tsp
Salt to taste
Sugar 5 gms / 1 tsp
Turmeric *(haldi)* powder 5 gms / 1 tsp

Method

1 Heat oil in a saucepan, sauté chopped onion, garlic paste and ground cloves. Fry lightly, add flour, turmeric, chilli, sugar and cinnamon. Cook gently for a few minutes.

2 Gradually add stock and creamed coconut to the pan and bring to boil stirring constantly. Reduce heat and simmer for 10 minutes.

3 Add the prawns and lemon juice. Season with salt, cook for another ten minutes.

4 Serve hot, accompanied by any Indian bread.

PRAWN CURRY

Serves: 4

Preparation time: 45 minutes

Cooking time: 35 minutes

TANDOORI LOBSTER

Ingredients

Lobster (medium) 4
Ginger paste (pg. 105) 20 gms / 4 tsp
Garlic paste (pg. 105) 20 gms / 4 tsp
Carom seeds *(ajwain)* 3 gms / ½ tsp
Vinegar, malt 120 ml / ½ cup
Salt to taste
Yoghurt, drained 200 gms / 1 cup
White pepper powder 5 gms / 1 tsp
Garam masala (pg. 105) 10 gms / 2 tsp
Egg 1
Cottage cheese *(paneer)* 60 gms / 4 tbs
Gramflour *(besan)* 45 gms / 3 tbs
Mustard oil 50 ml / 4 tbs
Red chilli paste 5 gms / 1 tsp
Butter for basting 100 gms / ½ cup

Method

1 Cut each lobster shell into half, then shell and devein the lobster. Wash and dry the shells, dip them in hot oil drain and keep aside.

2 Marinate the lobsters in a mixture made of ginger and garlic pastes, carom seeds, vinegar and salt. Keep aside for 1 hour.

3 Whisk yoghurt in a large bowl, add the remaining ingredients and coat the lobsters with this mixture. Keep aside for 3 hours.

4 Skewer the lobsters 2 cm apart. Keep a tray underneath to collect the excess drippings.

5 Roast in a moderately hot tandoor or pre-heated oven of 175 °C (350 °F) for 5 minutes.

6 Baste with butter and cook again for 2 minutes.

7 Place the lobster on the shell, garnish with lettuce, tomato slices and onion rings. Serve hot.

TANDOORI LOBSTER

Serves: 4-5

Preparation time: 5 hours

Cooking time: 10 minutes

Goan Fish Curry

Ingredients

Pomfret cut into pieces 600 gms
Salt to taste
Lemon juice 60 ml / 4 tbs
Coconut, grated 160 gms / ¾ cup
Red chillies, whole 15
Cumin *(jeera)* seeds 5 gms / 1 tsp
Coriander seeds 15 gms / 1 tbs
Turmeric *(haldi)* powder 5 gms / 1 tsp
Tamarind *(imlee)*, deseeded
45 gms / 3 tbs
Ginger paste (pg. 105) 20 gms / 4 tsp
Garlic paste (pg. 105) 5 gms / 1 tsp
Coconut milk 160 ml / ¾ cup
Groundnut oil 60 ml / 4 tbs
Onions, chopped 60 gms / 4 tbs
Green chillies 4
Tomatoes, chopped 60 gms / 4 tbs
Water 240 ml / 1¼ cup

Method

1 Sprinkle salt and lemon juice on the fish, marinate for an hour.

2 Blend the coconut, red chillies, cumin seeds, coriander seeds, turmeric powder, tamarind and the ginger and garlic pastes together with the coconut milk.

3 Heat oil in a *kadhai* (wok). Add the onions and sauté till golden brown. Add tomatoes and cook for 3 to 4 minutes or until the tomatoes are mashed.

4 Add the blended mixture and water, bring to a boil. Mix in green chillies and the fish, simmer for 7 minutes. Bring to a boil and then let simmer for 2 minutes. Do not cover the pot at any stage while the curry is being cooked.

5 Remove to a bowl and serve hot, accompanied by boiled rice.

GOAN FISH CURRY

Serves: 4

Preparation time: 1 hour

Cooking time: 30 minutes

Fish Curry in Mustard Oil

Ingredients

Pomfret 900 gms
Turmeric *(haldi)* powder 5 gms / 1 tsp
Salt 10 gms / 2 tsp
Mustard oil for frying
Fenugreek *(methi dana)* seeds 3 gms / ½ tsp
Cumin *(jeera)* seeds 3 gms / ½ tsp
Bayleaves *(tej patta)* 4
Onions, finely chopped 200 gms / 1 cup
Ginger-garlic paste (pg. 105) 20 gms / 4 tsp
Tomatoes, finely chopped 100 gms / ½ cup
Green chillies, sliced 10 gms / 2 tsp
Red chilli powder 5 gms / 1 tsp
Coriander powder 6 gms / 1 tsp
Water 500 ml / 2 ½ cups
Green coriander, chopped 5 gms / 1 tsp

Method

1 Wash and clean the fish, remove the head and tail and cut into pieces.

2 Apply half of turmeric powder and salt on the fish pieces and keep aside.

3 Heat mustard oil in a pan and shallow fry the fish on both sides till ¾ done. Remove and keep aside.

4 In the same pan, add fenugreek and cumin seeds, sauté till they crackle, add bayleaves, onions and stir-fry to a golden brown colour on medium heat.

5 Add the ginger-garlic paste, stir-fry for a minute, add tomatoes and cook till the oil separates.

6 Add green chillies, remaining salt, red chilli powder and coriander powder.

7 Cook on a low heat for 2-3 minutes, increase heat, add water and bring to a boil.

8 Add the fish pieces and simmer.

9 Cover and cook for 10-15 minutes, till the fish is completely cooked and the curry has thickened.

10 Remove from heat onto a serving dish and serve hot, garnished with chopped coriander.

Fish Curry in Mustard Oil

Serves: 4

Preparation time: 20 minutes

Cooking time: 40 minutes

FISH MOILEE

Ingredients

Fish fillets 600 gms
Oil 50 ml / 3 ⅔ tbs
Green cardamom (choti elaichi) 6
Curry leaves 2
Green chillies, slit 4-5
Ginger, chopped 10 gms / 2 tsp
Garlic, chopped 15 gms / 1 tbs
Onions, chopped 100 gms
Turmeric *(haldi)* powder 3 gms / ½ tsp
Coconut milk 500 ml / 2½ cups
Salt to taste

Method

1 Heat oil in a wok *(kadhai)*, add cardamom, curry leaves, green chillies, ginger and garlic, stir-fry for a minute. Add onions, sauté till transparent.

2 Stir in turmeric, fish fillets and coconut milk, cook for 15-20 minutes.

3 Season with salt, bring to boil and simmer for 8-10 minutes or until the fish is cooked.

4 Transfer to a serving dish and serve hot, accompanied by steamed rice and green salad.

Fish Moilee

Serves: 4-5

Preparation time:
10-15 minutes

Cooking time: 30-40 minutes

Fish Rolls

Ingredients

Fish (2" x 4" strips). 12
Butter 60 ml / 4 tbs
Onions, chopped 4
Green chilli, slit 3
Ginger, chopped 10 gms
Turmeric *(haldi)* powder 2 gms / ½ tsp
Yoghurt, whisked 200 ml / 1 cup
Cream 100 ml / ½ cup
Fenugreek *(methi dana)* seeds broiled, powdered 3 gms / ½ tsp
Green cardamom *(choti elaichi)* powder 3 gms / ½ tsp

Method

1 Roll each fish strip and secure with a toothpick.

2 Heat butter in a heavy bottomed pan and sauté onions untill soft.

3 Add green chillies and ginger to the onions and stir-fry for a few minutes.

4 Add turmeric powder, yoghurt, cream, fenugreek and green cardamom powder, sauté for 10-15 minutes.

5 Place the fish rolls in the sauce and cook on slow fire/dum for 10-15 minutes or until fish is cooked. Remove from heat.

6 Transfer the fish onto a serving dish, remove the toothpicks.

7 Strain the gravy and pour on top of the fish. Serve hot, garnished with green coriander and accompanied by steamed rice.

Fish Rolls

Serves: 4

Preparation time: 30 minutes

Cooking time: 45 minutes

Cottage Cheese and Capsicum Delight

Ingredients

Cottage cheese *(paneer)*, small cubes
600 gms
Capsicum *(green pepper)*
150 gms / ¾ cup
Tomatoes 150 gms / ¾ cup
Onions 150 gms / ¾ cup
Oil 60 ml / 4 tbs
Green cardamoms 3
Cumin seeds *(jeera)* 3 gms / ½ tsp
Turmeric powder *(haldi)* 8 gms / 1½ tsp
Red chilli powder 5 gms / 1 tsp
Garam masala (pg. 105) 15 gms / 1 tbs
Salt for seasoning
Green coriander, chopped 15 gms / 1 tbs
Lemon juice 10 ml / 2 tsp

Method

1 Dice the capsicum, tomatoes and onions into small pieces.

2 Heat the oil in a pan. Add the green cardamoms and cumin seeds and sauté over medium heat until they begin to crackle.

3 Add the turmeric powder and red chilli powder and sauté for 30 seconds.

4 Add the capsicum, onions and tomatoes and sauté for another 30 seconds over high heat.

5 Add paneer pieces, garam masala and salt. Sauté for 30 seconds, cover and cook for 6 minutes.

6 Sprinkle with green coriander and lemon juice before serving.

Cottage Cheese and Capsicum Delight

Serves: 4-5

Preparation time: 15 minutes

Cooking time: 15 minutes

Lotus Stems in an Exotic Curry

Ingredients

Lotus stem *(kamal kakri)* 800 gms
Mustard oil 250 gms / 1¼ cups
Water
Cloves *(laung)* 2
Green cardamoms *(choti elaichi)* 2
Fennel *(saunf)* powder 30 gms / 2 tbs
Salt 5 gms / 1 tsp
Cumin *(jeera)* powder 2 gms / ⅓ tsp
Cinnamon *(daalchini)* powder 3 gms / ½ tsp
Black cardamom *(bari elaichi)* powder 6 gms / 1 tsp
Yoghurt, whisked 1-500 kg / 7½ cups

Method

1 Scrape away the skin of the lotus stems. Cut into 1½" long pieces, discarding the ends. Wash well and drain.

2 Heat the mustard oil in a *kadhai* (wok) and deep fry the lotus stems till they are half cooked. Drain and keep aside.

3 To the same *kadhai* (wok), add water and the lotus stems, bring to a boil, add all the spices, mix in the yoghurt. Cook till the curry thickens and the lotus stems are tender, stirring regularly.

4 Remove into a serving dish and serve hot.

LOTUS STEMS IN AN EXOTIC CURRY

Serves: 4

Preparation time: 10 minutes

Cooking time: 30 minutes

COTTAGE CHEESE COOKED IN A WOK

Ingredients

Cottage cheese *(paneer)* (pg. 105) 600 gms
Capsicum 45 gms / 3 tbs
Red chillies, whole 15
Coriander seeds 10 gms / 2 tsp
Oil 45 ml / 3 tbs
Onions, chopped 45 gms / 3 tbs
Ginger, julienned 15 gms / 1 tbs
Tomato purée (pg. 105) 150 ml / ¾ cup
Salt to taste
Fenugreek powder *(methi)* 5 gms / 1 tsp
Garam masala (pg. 105) 8 gms / 1½ tsp
Coriander powder 10 gms / 2 tsp
Black pepper 8 gms / 1½ tsp
Green coriander, chopped 15 gms / 1 tbs

Method

1 Cut the cottage cheese into fingers. Cut the capsicum into halves, deseed and make juliennes or cut into small, even squares.

2 Pound the red chillies and coriander seeds with a pestle to a powder.

3 Heat the oil in a *kadhai* (wok), sauté the onions and capsicum over medium heat for 2 minutes.

4 Add the pounded spices and two-thirds of the ginger, stir for 1 minute.

5 Add the tomato purée and salt, bring to a boil, simmer until the oil separates from the gravy.

6 Add the cottage cheese and stir gently for 2-3 minutes.

7 Stir in fenugreek powder, garam masala, coriander powder and black pepper.

8 Garnish with chopped coriander and the remaining julienned ginger. Serve hot, accompanied by Khasta Roti (page 86) and Boondi Raita (page 96).

COTTAGE CHEESE COOKED IN A WOK

Serves: 4

Preparation time: 15 minutes

Cooking time: 10 minutes

Mushroom and Corn Bonanza

Ingredients

Mushroom 500 gms
Sweet Corn 250 gms
Oil 75 ml / 5 tbs
Green cardamoms *(choti elaichi)* 4
Cloves *(laung)* 3
Ginger paste (pg. 105) 10 gms / 2 tsp
Garlic paste (pg. 105) 10 gms / 2 tsp
Mace *(javitri)* powder a pinch
Onion paste (pg. 105) 100 gms / ½ cup
Cashewnut paste 45 gms / 3 tbs
Yoghurt 250 gms / 1¼ cup
Green chilli, slit 4
Salt to taste
Cream 100 ml / ½ cup
Green coriander, chopped
45 gms / 3 tbs

Method

1 Heat oil in a heavy bottomed pan.

2 Add green cardamom, cloves and mace powder. As it crackles, add ginger and garlic pastes.

3 Stir-fry for few minutes. Add onion paste and cashew paste.

4 Stir-fry for 5-6 minutes. Add yogurt, slit green chillies and salt.

5 Add mushroom and corn, simmer for 20 minutes.

6 Stir in the cream, garnish with slit green chillies and serve at once, accompanied by Poori (page 24).

Mushroom and Corn Bonanza

Serves: 4-6

Preparation time: 15 minutes

Cooking time: 30 minutes

Stir-fried Mushrooms

Ingredients

Mushrooms ½ kg
Coriander leaves, chopped 15 gms / 1 tbs
Garam masala (pg. 105) 3 gms / ½ tsp
Garlic paste (pg. 105) 5 gms / 1 tsp
Oil 22 ml / 4½ tsp
Onions, sliced 2
Red chilli powder 3 gms / ½ tsp
Salt to taste
Tomato, chopped 1
Turmeric *(haldi)* powder 3 gms / ½ tsp

Method

1 Cut mushrooms in slices.

2 Heat oil and fry onions until golden in colour. Add garlic paste and chopped tomatoes, mix well.

3 Put in turmeric, garam masala, chilli powder, salt and fry for 3-4 mins. Stir in mushrooms and simmer until mushrooms are tender, adding very little water if necessary.

4 Garnish with coriander and serve hot.

STIR-FRIED MUSHROOMS

Serves: 4

Preparation time: 10 minutes

Cooking time: 20 minutes

Mushrooms in Tomato Gravy

Ingredients

Mushrooms,without stems, boiled
600 gms
Oil 100 ml / ½ cup
Bayleaves *(tej patta)* 4
Mace *(javitri)* 3 gms / ½ tsp
Cloves *(laung)* 4
Green cardamom *(choti elaichi)* 4
Black cardamom *(bari elaichi)* 4
Cinnamon *(daalchini)* sticks, small 2
Ginger-garlic paste (pg. 105)
20 gms / 4 tsp
Tomato purée, fresh (pg. 105)
300 gms / 1½ cups
Salt to taste
Red chilli powder 10 gms / 2 tsp
Turmeric *(haldi)* powder 5 gms / 1 tsp
Coriander powder 10 gms / 2 tsp
Brown onion paste (pg. 105)
150 gms / 3/4 cup
Yoghurt, whisked 45 gms / 3 tbs
Water 100 ml / ½ cup
Garam masala (pg. 105) a pinch
Green coriander, chopped 5 gms / 1 tsp
Ginger, julienned 5 gms / 1 tsp
Green chillies, julienned 5 gms / 1 tsp

Method

1 Heat oil in a *handi* (pot), add bayleaves, mace, cloves, green cardamom, black cardamom and cinnamom, sauté till they crackle.

2 Stir in ginger-garlic paste dissolved in a little water and stir-fry till the water dries out.

3 Add tomato purée, salt, red chilli powder, turmeric powder, coriander powder and sauté for 2-3 minutes till the oil seperates.

4 Add the brown onion paste and yoghurt, stir-fry for 2-3 minutes, add the mushrooms alongwith water. Cook on low heat until the curry thickens and the mushrooms are cooked. Remove from heat and transfer to a serving dish.

5 Serve hot, garnished with garam masala, green coriander, julienned ginger and green chillies.

Mushrooms in Tomato Gravy

Serves: 4

Preparation time: 40 minutes

Cooking time: 30 minutes

Potato Curry

Ingredients

Potatoes (small) 600 gms
Oil 100 ml / ½ cup
Onions, chopped 20 gms / 4 tsp
Cumin *(jeera)* seeds 10 gms / 2 tsp
Turmeric *(haldi)* powder 3 gms / ½ tsp
Red chilli powder 5 gms / 1 tsp
Cumin *(jeera)* powder 10 gms / 2 tsp
Cashewnut paste (optional) 30 gms / 2 tbs
Cloves *(laung)* powder 3 gms / ½ tsp
Cinnamon *(daalchini)* powder a pinch
Salt to taste
Yoghurt 400 gms / 2 cups

Method

1 Peel the potatoes and soak in water.

2 Heat oil (1 tbs) in a pan and sauté onions till brown.

3 Heat oil in a *kadhai* (wok), sauté cumin seeds till they crackle, add turmeric powder, red chilli powder and cumin powder alongwith water (½ cup).

4 Mix in all the remaining ingredients and cook for 5 minutes.

5 Add the peeled potatoes to the curry, seal the lid with dough. Cook on low flame for 30-35 minutes.

6 Remove from heat, transfer to a serving dish and serve hot, accompanied by Naan (page 34) and Boondi Raita (page 96).

POTATO CURRY

Serves: 4

Preparation time: 15 minutes

Cooking time: 40 minutes

Crunchy Okra

Ingredients

Okra *(bhindi)* ½ kg
Carom *(ajwain)* seeds 3 gms / ½ tsp
Chaat masala 3 gms / ½ tsp
Garam masala (pg. 105) 5 gms / 1 tsp
Ginger, julienned 7 gms / 1½ tsp
Gramflour *(besan)* 45 gms / 3 tbs
Green chillies, sliced (optional) 2
Oil for frying
Raw mango *(amchoor)* powder
3 gms / ½ tsp
Red chillies 5 gms / 1 tsp
Salt to taste

Method

1 Snip off both ends of each okra, slice lengthwise into four slices.

2 Spread all sliced okra on a flat dish and sprinkle evenly with salt, chilli powder, garam masala, mango powder and chaat masala. Mix gently to coat okra evenly.

3 Now sprinkle gramflour over the okra and mix in so they are coated evenly, without adding any water preferably.

4 Divide the okra into two portions. Heat oil in a *kadhai* (wok) or a pan till it is smoking. Fry one portion coated okra slices, separating each lightly with a fork. Do not allow slices to stick to each other.

5 Remove from oil when both sides are crispy and brown in colour. Fry the other portion in the same way and serve at once.

6 Garnish with julienned ginger and green chillies and serve hot.

CRUNCHY OKRA

Serves: 4-6

Preparation time: 40 minutes

Cooking time: 30 minutes

Spiced Cauliflower

Ingredients

Cauliflower, small, whole 5
Oil for frying
Onions, chopped
200 gms / 1 cup
Cashewnuts 100 gms / ½ cup
Green cardamoms (choti elaichi) 6
Turmeric *(haldi)* powder 5 gms / 1 tsp
Red chilli powder 10 gms / 2 tsp
Ginger paste (pg. 105) 25 gms / 5 tsp
Garlic paste (pg. 105) 25 gms / 5 tsp
Garam masala (pg. 105) 10 gms / 2 tsp
Yoghurt, whisked 200 gms / 1 cup
Salt to taste
Butter 30 gms / 2 tbs
Lemon juice 15 ml / 1 tbs
Mace *(javitri)* powder 3 gms / ½ tsp

Method

1 Wash, clean and remove the stems of the cauliflower.

2 Heat oil in a *kadhai* (wok), deep fry each cauliflower over medium heat until almost cooked.

3 In the same oil, fry onions and cashewnuts (saving a few for garnishing), grind to a fine paste.

4 Heat oil (5 tbs) in a pan, add cardamoms, sauté for a few seconds. Add turmeric powder, red chilli powder, ginger-garlic pastes and garam masala, cook for 30 seconds.

5 Add onions-cashewnut paste and whisked yoghurt, cook for 10 minutes on low heat and season to taste with salt.

6 Arrange the fried cauliflower in a baking dish and pour the curry over each cauliflower. Bake in a moderate oven of 175 °C (350 °F) for 10 minutes.

7 Garnish with fried cashewnuts, dot with melted butter and sprinkle lemon juice and mace powder. Serve hot, accompanied by Khasta Roti (page 86).

SPICED CAULIFLOWER

Serves: 4-5

Preparation time: 10 minutes

Cooking time: 45 minutes

CRISPY CAULIFLOWER

Ingredients

Cauliflower, 5 small whole ones 1 kg
Carom *(ajwain)* seeds 6 gms / 1 tsp
Garam masala (pg. 105) 8 gms / 1 ⅔ tsp
Garlic paste (pg. 105) 10 gms / 2 tsp
Ginger paste (pg. 105) 10 gms / 2 tsp
Gramflour *(besan)* / White flour / Maize flour *(makke ka atta)* 200 gms / 1 cup
Green chillies, finely chopped 20 gms / 4 tsp
Green coriander, finely chopped 20 gms / 4 tsp
Lemon juice 3 ml / ⅔ tsp
Oil 500 ml / 2½ cups
Red or Yellow chilli powder 10 gms / 2 tsp
Salt to taste
Turmeric *(haldi)* powder 10 gms / 2 tsp
Yoghurt 100 gms / ½ cup

Method

1 Boil sufficient water to immerse the cauliflowers. Add salt and turmeric powder.

2 Gradually add the cauliflowers to this brine solution. Cook for 8-10 minutes over medium heat until the cauliflowers are half cooked. Drain and keep aside.

3 In a bowl make a batter with the gramflour *(besan)*/white flour, carom seeds, lemon juice, yoghurt, ginger, garlic pastes, garam masala, chilli powder and salt. The batter consistency should be thick and smooth.

4 Heat the oil in a *kadhai* (wok). Dip each cauliflower into the batter, coat evenly and deep fry over medium heat till golden.

5 Cut each cauliflower in four and serve on a platter, garnished with green coriander and green chillies. Serve with fresh cucumbers, sliced tomatoes and Mint Chutney (page 102).

Crispy Cauliflower

Serves: 4-5

Preparation time: 15 minutes

Cooking time: 15 minutes

Minced Peas and Potatoes

Ingredients

Peas, minced 300 gms / 1½ cup
Potatoes (small), diced 5-6
Green chillies, chopped 1-2
Ginger, peeled and chopped 1½" piece
Tomatoes, chopped 400 gms /2 cups
Clarified butter *(ghee)* 100 ml / ½ cup
Cumin *(jeera)* seeds 5 gms / 1½ tsp
Cloves *(laung)*, ground 6
Cinnamon *(daalchini)* sticks (1"), ground 2
Peppercorns, ground 6-8
Coriander powder 15 gms / 1 tbs
Turmeric *(haldi)* powder 5 gms / 1 tsp
Red chilli powder 3 gms / ½ tsp
Salt to taste
Coriander, fresh 30 gms / 2 tbs
Garam masala (pg. 105) 15 gms / 1 tbs

Method

1 Blend the green chillies, ginger and tomatoes to a purée. Set aside.

2 Heat clarified butter (60 ml / 4 tbs) in a *kadhai* (wok) and brown the minced peas till the oil separates. Set aside.

3 Heat clarified butter (1 tbs), add the cumin seeds, fry for a few seconds. Add the browned peas paste, cloves, cinnamon, peppercorns, ground coriander, turmeric powder, red chilli powder and cook for a few minutes.

4 Stir in the green chillies, ginger and tomato purée, bring to a boil.

5 Mix in the diced potatoes and cook till potatoes become tender.

6 Season with salt and garam masala, garnish with chopped coriander and serve hot.

MINCED PEAS AND POTATOES

Serves: 4-6

Preparation time: 10 minutes

Cooking time: 30 minutes

Pomegranate Potatoes

Ingredients

Potatoes, boiled, cut into 1½" cubes 1 kg
Pomegranate *(anar dana)* seeds, dried, crushed 200 gms / 1 cup
Butter 100 gms / ½ cup
Coriander powder 15 gms / 1 tbs
Turmeric *(haldi)* powder 3 gms / ½ tsp
Red chilli powder 6 gms / 1 tsp
Salt to taste
Green chillies, slit 6
Green coriander, chopped 20 gms / 4 tsp

Method

1 Heat butter in a heavy bottomed pan. Add coriander powder, turmeric powder, red chilli powder and half of the pomegranate seeds and stir.

2 Mix in the potatoes. Sprinkle salt and green chillies. Mix gently, so the spices coat the potatoes evenly, reduce heat and simmer for 10-15 minutes. Remove from heat.

3 Serve hot, garnished with chopped coriander and remaining pomegranate seeds.

POMEGRANATE POTATOES

Serves: 4

Preparation time: 30 minutes

Cooking time: 15-20 minutes

Tangy Aubergines

Ingredients

Aubergine *(baigan)* 800 gms
Tamarind *(imlee)* 75 gms / 5 tbs
Mustard oil 250 ml / 1 ¼ cup
Cloves *(laung)* 2
Green cardamom *(choti elaich)* 2
Green chillies, slit 4
Red chilli powder 20 gms / 4 tsp
Water, hot 400 ml / 2 cups
Salt to taste
Turmeric *(haldi)* powder a pinch
Black cardamom *(bari elaichi)* powder 3 gms / ½ tsp
Fennel *(saunf)* powder 30 gms / 2 tbs
Cinnamon *(daalchini)* powder 3 gms / ½ tsp
Cumin *(jeera)* powder 3 gms / ½ tsp

Method

1 Clean and cut the aubergines into guarters lengthwise.

2 Soak tamarind in sufficient water. Extract the tamarind juice and discard the seeds.

3 Heat mustard oil in a *handi* (pot) and fry the aubergines till half cooked. Remove, drain excess oil and keep aside.

4 Add cloves and green cardamom in the remaining oil and sauté till they crackle, add green chillies and sauté further for a minutes.

5 Stir in the red chilli powder, water (2 cups), salt, turmeric powder and the remaining spices. Bring to a boil and add the tamarind extract. Cook for 3-5 minutes till the curry begins to thicken.

6 Add the fried aubergines. Cover and cook on low heat till the curry has thickened and the aubergines are tender.

7 Remove from heat, transfer to a serving dish and serve hot, accompanied by a green salad and any Indian bread.

TANGY AUBERGINES

Serves: 4

Preparation time: 30 minutes

Cooking time: 30 minutes

Garam masala

Khoya

Onion paste

BROCCOLI AND CARROT PULAO

Serves: 4-5

Preparation time: 5 minutes

Cooking time: 30 minutes

Lamb Biryani

Ingredients

Lamb (cut into 1" cubes) 1 kg
Basmati rice 400 gms / 2 cups
Oil 100 ml / ½ cup
Onions, chopped 120 gms / ½ cup
Green cardamoms *(choti elaichi)* 5
Cloves *(laung)* 2
Cinnamon *(daalchini)* stick (1") 1
Yoghurt, whisked 120 gms / ½ cup
Yellow chilli powder 5 gms / 1 tsp
Salt to taste
Lamb stock 400 ml / 2 cups
Mace *(javitri)* powder a pinch
Mint leaves, chopped 5 gms / 1 tsp
Ginger, chopped 30 gms / 2 tbs
Vetivier *(kewda)* a few drops
Cream 120 ml / ½ cup
Butter, melted 45 gms / 3 tbs
Saffron *(kesar)* a pinch
Dough to seal dish
Ginger, julienned 5 gms / 1 tsp

Method

1 Heat oil in a pan and sauté chopped onions. Add cardamoms, cloves and cinnamon in the oil till they crackle, then add lamb pieces and sauté.

2 Add yoghurt, yellow chilli powder and salt. Stir till dry. Add stock and cook till meat is almost done.

3 In a separate pan, boil rice in plenty of water till the grains lengthen but are not fully cooked. Drain the water.

4 Remove meat pieces from curry and spread in a heat-proof casserole. Strain the curry. Reserve half of the curry and pour the remaining onto the meat. Sprinkle mace, mint, chopped ginger, vetivier and half the cream over the meat.

5 Place half the rice on the meat pieces. Sprinkle reserved cream, the reserved liquid, melted butter and saffron, crushed in a spoonful of water over it.

6 Place rest of the rice on top. Cover and seal lid with dough. Cook over very gentle heat for about 10-15 minutes. Remove from heat, garnish with julienned ginger.

7 Serve hot, accompanied by Mixed Vegetable Raita (page 94).

LAMB BIRYANI

Serves: 4

Preparation time: 30 minutes

Cooking time: 1 hour
30 minutes

LEMON RICE

Ingredients

Rice, basmati or any
long grain variety 100 gms / ½ cup
Lemon juice 80 ml / ⅓ cup
Water 400-480 ml / 2-2⅔ cups
Salt 5 gms / 1 tsp
Oil/Clarified butter *(ghee)* 45 ml / 3 tbs
Cashewnuts, chopped 75 gms / ½ cup
Lentils *(urad daal)*, split 7 gms / ½ tbs
Mustard *(raee)* seeds 5 gms / 1 tsp
Red chillies, whole 2-3
Turmeric *(haldi)* powder 3 gms / ½ tsp
Coriander, coarsely chopped
45 gms / 3 tbs
Coconut, fresh, shredded
25 gms / ¼ cup

Method

1 Wash and soak the rice in water for 10 minutes. Drain and keep aside.

2 Boil water in a heavy pan. Stir in rice, salt and oil (7 ml / ½ tbs). Cover tightly, reduce heat and simmer without stirring until rice is fluffy and tender and water is fully absorbed. Keep aside.

3 Heat remaining oil in a small pan, stir-fry the cashewnuts until golden brown. Drain excess oil and spoon cashewnuts over the cooked rice. Replace cover.

4 Raise the heat slightly, sauté the lentils and mustard seeds till the lentils turn reddish brown, mustard seeds splutter and add whole red chillies and remove from heat.

5 Gently fold in the lentils, turmeric, lime juice, coriander and coconut into the cooked rice until well mixed.

6 Serve hot, accompanied by plain yoghurt.

LEMON RICE

Serves: 4

Preparation time: 5 minutes

Cooking time: 25-35 minutes

Chicken Biryani

Ingredients

Chicken (cut into 1" cubes) 1 kg
Basmati rice 400 gms / 2 cups
Butter, melted 45 gms / 3 tbs
Green cardamoms *(choti elaichi)* 5
Cinnamon stick (1") 1
Cloves *(laung)* 2
Cooking oil 100 ml / ½ cup
Cream 120 ml / ½ cup
Dough to seal dish
Ginger, chopped 30 gms / 2 tbs
Ginger, julienned 5 gms / 1 tsp
Chicken stock 400 ml / 2 cups
Mace *(javitri)* powder a pinch
Mint leaves, chopped 5 gms / 1 tsp
Onions, chopped 120 gms / ½ cup
Saffron a pinch
Salt to taste
Vetivier *(kewda)* a few drops
Yellow chilli powder 5 gms / 1 tsp
Yoghurt 120 gms / ½ cup

Method

1 Heat oil in a pan and sauté chopped onions. Add cardamoms, cloves and cinnamon in the oil till they crackle, then add chicken pieces and sauté.

2 Add yoghurt, yellow chilli powder and salt. Stir till dry. Add stock and cook till meat is almost done.

3 In a separate pan, boil rice in plenty of water till the grains lengthen but are not fully cooked. Drain the water.

4 Remove meat pieces from curry and spread in a heat-proof casserole. Strain curry. Reserve half and pour the remainder onto the meat. Sprinkle mace, mint, chopped ginger, vetivier and half the cream over the meat.

5 Place half the rice on the meat pieces. Sprinkle reserved cream, the reserved liquid, melted butter and saffron, crushed in a spoonful of water over it.

6 Place rest of the rice on top. Cover and seal lid with dough. Cook over very gentle heat for about 10-15 minutes. Serve hot, accompanied by Irani Raita (page 98).

CHICKEN BIRYANI

Serves: 4

Preparation time: 30 minutes

Cooking time: 1 hour 30 minutes

Prawn Biryani

Ingredients

Prawns, shelled, deveined 100 gms
Basmati rice 350 gms / 1¾ cup
Water 400 ml / 2 cups
Salt to taste
Turmeric powder *(haldi)* a pinch
Lemon 1
Oil 15 ml / 1 tbs
Cinnamon *(daalchini)* stick 1
Green cardamom *(choti elaichi)* 4
Black cardamom *(bari elaichi)* 2
Cloves *(laung)* 4
Bayleaves *(tej patta)* 4
Onions, sliced 45 gms / 3 tbs
Ginger-garlic paste (pg. 105) 10 gms / 2 tsp
Vegetable stock 750 litre / 3 ¾ cup
Salt 8 gms / 1½ tsp
Butter 100 gms / ½ cup
Milk 45 ml / 3 tbs

Method

1 Pick, wash and soak the rice for ½ hour. Drain and keep aside.

2 Take water in a pan, add salt to taste, turmeric powder and lemon juice. Bring to a boil and add the prawns. Cook till prawns are ¾ done. Remove, cut into small pieces, keep aside.

3 Heat oil in a *handi* (pot). Add the whole spices, and sauté till they crackle, add the sliced onions and stir-fry to a golden brown. Add ginger-garlic paste dissolved in a little water.

4 Add the vegetable stock and bring to a boil. Add salt, butter (90 gms) and lemon juice.

5 Add the drained rice and cook on a medium heat, stirring occasionally.

6 When the water has reduced to the level of rice, sprinkle milk on top and cover with a wet cloth.

7 Put on very low heat *(dum)* for approx 15 minutes or till cooked. Remove from heat.

8 Heat the remaining butter and sauté the prawn pieces for a minute.

9 Transfer the rice to a serving dish and serve hot, garnished with prawns and accompanied by Boondi Raita (page 96).

PRAWN BIRYANI

Serves: 4

Preparation time: 1 hour

Cooking time: 25 minutes

JACKFRUIT PULAO

Ingredients

Basmati rice 200 gms / 1 cup
Jackfruit (cleaned, and cubed) 250 gms / 1½ cup
Bayleaf *(tej patta)* 1
Black cardamoms *(bari elaichi)* 2
Black cumin *(shah jeera)* 5 gms / 1 tsp
Cinnamon stick (medium) 1
Cloves *(laung)* 4
Ginger paste (pg. 105) 10 gms / 2 tsp
Oil 200 ml / 1 cup
Onions, chopped 50 gms / ¼ cup
Red chilli powder 3 gms / ½ tsp
Salt to taste
Water 500 ml / 2½ cups
White pepper powder 3 gms / ½ tsp

For the garnishing:

Cashewnuts, sliced and fried 5 gms / 1 tsp
Coriander, chopped 3 gms / ½ tsp
Cream 30 ml / 2 tbs
Ginger, julienned 3 gms / ½ tsp
Green chillies, sliced and deseeded 5 gms/ 1 tsp
Lemon juice 15 ml / 1 tbs
Mace power *(javitri)* 3 gms / ½ tsp
Onion, sliced and fried 1

Method

1 Clean, wash and soak the rice for 30 minutes.

2 Heat oil in a *kadhai* (wok) till it smoking. Fry jackfruit cubes till light brown in colour. Drain oil from them and keep aside.

3 Reheat same oil in a heavy pan, add the cloves, cinnamon stick, bay leaf, cardamom and cumin seeds, saute over medium heat until they begin to crackle.

4 Add chopped onions and sauté. Stir in the ginger paste and red chilli powder. Add the fried jackfruit, white pepper powder and salt. Cook for 3-4 minutes.

5 Stir in water alongwith drained rice. Bring to a boil, reduce heat and cook till rice is done.

6 Remove lid and sprinkle ginger, slit green chillies, onions, mace powder, lemon juice, cashewnut, green coriander and cream.

7 Seal lid with dough, cook on very low heat for 10-15 minutes.

Serve hot, accompanied by Orange Raita (page 96).

JACKFRUIT PULAO

Serves: 4-5

Preparation time: 45 minutes

Cooking time: 30 minutes

Mushroom Pulao

Ingredients

Black mushrooms *(gucchi)* 30 gms
Basmati rice 350 gms / 1 3/4 cup
Oil 15 ml /1 tbs
Cinnaman *(dalchinni)* sticks 1
Green cardamom *(choti elaichi)* 4
Black cardamom *(bari elaichi)* 2
Cloves *(laung)* 4
Bayleaves *(tej patta)* 4
Onion, sliced 45 gms / 3 tsp
Ginger-garlic paste (pg. 105) 10 gms /2 tsp
Vegetable stock 750 ml / 3 3/4 cup
Salt to taste
Butter 100 gms / ½ cup
Lemon ½
Milk 60 ml / 4 tbs

Method

1 Soak the black mushrooms and basmati rice in separate pans for 30 minutes. Drain and keep aside.

2 Cut the black mushrooms into small pieces.

3 Heat oil in a *handi* (pot), add the whole spices, saute till they crackle, add the onions and stir-fry till golden brown in colour.

4 Add ginger, garlic paste dissolved in a little water and saute further.

5 Stir in the vegetable stock and bring to a boil. Add salt, butter (90 gms) and lemon juice.

6 Add the rice and cook on medium heat, stirring occasionally. When water reduces to the level of rice, sprinkle milk on top and cover with a wet cloth. Cook on very low heat for 15 minutes or until the rice is cooked.

7 Heat remaining butter in a pan and saute blace mushrooms for a few minutes. Remove from heat and keep aside.

8 Remove the prepared rice to a serving dish and serve hot, garnished with fried mushrooms.

MUSHROOM PULAO

Serves: 2

Preparation time: 1 hour

Cooking time: 30-40 minutes

Cottage Cheese Pulao

Ingredients

Cottage cheese *(paneer)* 80 gms
Cornflour 10 gms / 2 tsp
Salt to taste
Red chilli powder 3 gms / ½ tsp
Oil 15 ml / 1 tbs + for frying
Basmati rice 350 gms /1 ¾ cup
Ginger-garlic paste (pg. 105) 45 gms / 3 tbs
Cinnamon *(dalchinni)* powder
10 gms / 2 tsp
Green cardamom *(choti elaichi)* 4
Black cardamom *(bari elaichi)* 2
Cloves *(laung)* 4
Bayleaves *(tej patta)* 4
Vegetable stock 750 ml / 3 ¾ cup
Butter 100 gms / ½ cup
Lemon ½
Salt 8 gms / 1½ tsp
Milk 60 ml / 4 tbs
Onion, sliced 45 gms / 3 tbs

Method

1 Soak rice in sufficient water for 30 minutes, drain and keep aside.

2 Mash the cottage cheese, add salt to taste, red chilli powder and cornflour. Mix well and make small balls of the cottage cheese mixture. Heat oil in a pan and deep fry to a light golden brown colour. Remove and keep aside.

3 Heat oil in a *handi* (pot), add the whole spices and saute till they crackle, add sliced onions and stir-fry to a golden brown colour. Add ginger-garlic paste dissolved in water.

4 Stir vegetable stock and bring to a boil. Add salt (8 gms), butter and lemon juice. Add the rice and cook on medium heat, stirring occasionally.

5 When water reduces to the level of rice sprinkle milk on top, cover with wet cloth and cook on very low heat *(dum)* for 15 minutes or until the rice is cooked.

6 Remove from heat and serve hot, garnished with fried cottage cheese balls.

COTTAGE CHEESE PULAO

Serves: 4

Preparation time: 1 hour

Cooking time: 25 minutes

POORI

Ingredients

Whole wheat flour 250 gms / 1¼ cups
Oil 10 ml / 2 tsp
Oil for deep frying
Salt to taste
Water 125 ml / ½ cup

Method

1 Sieve the wheat flour and salt into a bowl. Add 10 ml of oil.

2 Make a well in the sieved flour, add cold water to it and gradually start mixing to form a fine hard dough.

3 Divide the dough into 25 equal size balls and place them on a lightly floured surface. Cover with a kitchen cloth for 5-10 minutes.

4 Flatten each ball between the palms to make a round, 4.5 cm in diameter. Roll out each of them to form an 6 cm disc.

5 Heat the oil and deep fry the pooris until they puff up.

6 Drain on a paper towel before serving. Serve hot, as an accompaniment to any Indian curry.

POORI

Unleavened puffed pancake—
a north Indian speciality

Serves: 4-5

Preparation time: 20 minutes

Cooking time: 10 minutes

BAKARKHANI

Ingredients

Plain flour 500 gms/2½ cups
Almonds, blanched and slivered
15 gms / 1 tbs
Baking powder 5 gms / 1 tsp
Dry yeast 8 gms / 1½ tsp
Flour to dust
Clarified butter *(ghee)* 150 gms/¾ cup
Green cardamom *(choti elaichi)* powder
3 gms / ½ tsp
Milk, warmed 250 gms / 1¼ cup
Raisins 15 gms / 3 tsp
Salt to taste
Sugar 15 gms / 3 tsp

Method

1 Sieve the flour, baking powder and salt in a mixing bowl.

2 Dissolve the sugar in warm milk and stir.

3 Dissolve the yeast in a little warm water and allow it to rise for 20 minutes.

4 Soak almonds in water along with the raisins for half an hour and then drain.

5 Make a well in the sieved flour and pour in the milk and dissolved yeast Knead to a smoothdough. Cover and keep aside for 5 minutes.

6 Add clarified butter and knead to a soft dough. Add almonds, raisins and cardamom powder, knead, cover and keep in a warm place for half an hour to allow the dough to rise.

7 Divide into 12 equal portions, make the dough balls, dust with flour, cover and keep aside for 10 minutes. Place the balls on a lightly floured surface and roll out into round discs, 8 cm in diameter. Prick the surfaces of the dough with a fork.

8 Heat the oven to 175 °C (350 °F). Grease a baking tray with ghee, arrange the rolled out discs on it and bake for 8-10 minutes.

9 Remove the Bakarkhani, brush with clarified butter and serve immediately.

BAKARKHANI

Bread with almonds and raisins

Serves: 4-5

Preparation time: 2 hours

Cooking time: 10 minutes

Khameeri Roti

Ingredients

Wholewheat flour 480 gms / 2 cups
Yeast, fresh 8 gms / 1½ tsp
Salt to taste
Flour to dust
Clarified butter *(ghee)* to grease baking tray.

Method

1 Dislove the yeast in (½ cup) warm water.

2 Sieve the flour with salt onto a platter.

3 Make a well in the flour and pour (1 cup) water. Mix flour and water gradually, then knead into a tough dough. Cover with a damp cloth and keep aside for 15 minutes.

4 Slowly sprinkle the dissolved yeast over the dough and keep kneading till the dough is smooth and pliable and not sticky. Cover with damp cloth and keep aside for 30 minutes.

5 Divide dough into 8 equal balls and dust with dry flour.

6 Press and flatten each ball into round discs, 8 inches wide. Wearing an oven glove stick the disc to the side of a hot tandoor and bake for 2 minutes. Remove with a pair of tongs. Alternatively, place on a greased baking tray and bake for 4-5 minutes in a preheated oven at 175 °C (350 °F).

7 Serve hot, as an accompaniment to any curry dish.

KHAMEERI ROTI

Leavened bread

Serves: 4

Preparation time: 1 hour

Cooking time: 4-5 minutes for each roti

Taftan

Ingredients

Rice flour 480 gms / 2 cups
Salt to taste
Water 120 ml / ½ cup
Sugar 3 gms / ½ tsp
Milk 240 ml / 1 cup
Clarified butter *(ghee)* 180 gms / ¾ cup
Yeast 3 gms / ½ tsp
Melon *(magaz)* seeds 10 gms / 2 tsp
Green coriander, chopped 10 gms / 2 tsp
Butter or clarified butter *(ghee)* for brushing

Method

1. Sieve flour and salt together.
2. Make a well in the flour and add water, sugar, milk, clarified butter *(ghee)*, yeast and melon seeds. Mix gradually and knead into a soft dough.
3. Divide into 4 equal balls and set aside for half an hour.
4. Dust lightly and roll into 3½ inch discs, a quarter of an inch thick. Sprinkle with coriander.
5. Put into tandoor and bake till brown in colour.
6. Brush with clarified butter *(ghee)* and serve hot.

TAFTAN

A rich, leavened, rice flour bread

Serves: 4

Preparation time: 1 hour

Cooking time: 10 minutes for each taftan

Lachha Parantha

Ingredients

Flour 480 gms / 2 1/3 cups
Fennel *(saunf)* 10 gms / 2 tsp
Clarified butter *(ghee)* 180 ml / ¾ cup
Clarified butter to shallow fry
Milk 240 ml / 1¼ cup
Salt to taste
Water 120 ml / ½ cup

Method

1 Pound fennel with a pestle.

2 Sieve flour and salt together. Make a well in the flour and pour in milk and water. Mix gradually and knead into a dough. Cover with moist cloth and keep aside for 10 min.

3 Melt 1/3 of the clarified butter, add to the dough, kneading constantly to make it soft and smooth.

4 Add pounded fennel and knead again for 5 minutes.

5 Divide into 12 equal balls, dust lightly, roll into 6" discs. Apply clarified butter 1 tsp evenly over one side.

6 Make a radial cut and fold disc into a narrow conical shape. Place flat side of the cone on palm and twist palms together in a round movement to compress dough into a thick flat round *(pedha)*. Dust with flour, roll it out into an 8 inch disc. Refrigerate for an hour on butter paper.

7 Heat griddle and shallow fry both sides over low heat till golden.

8 Serve hot, accompanied by any curry dish.

LACHHA PARANTHA

A multi-layered bread, flavoured with fennel

Serves: 4

Preparation time: 1 hour 30 minutes

Cooking time: 30 minutes

NAAN

Ingredients

Flour 500 gms / 2½ cups
Baking powder 5 gms / 1 tsp
Baking soda 3 gm / ½ tsp
Clarified butter *(ghee)*/Oil 25 ml / 5 tsp
Egg 1
Melon *(magaz)* seeds 5 gms / 1 tsp
Milk 60 ml / 4 tbs
Onion *(kalonji)* seeds 3 gms / ½ tsp
Salt to taste
Sugar 10 gms / 2 tsp

Method

1 Sieve the flour, salt, baking soda and baking powder into a bowl. Add enough water to make a hard dough.

2 Whisk egg, sugar and milk in a bowl and knead into the dough to make it soft and smooth. Cover with moist cloth, keep aside for 10 minutes.

3 Add oil, knead and punch the dough, cover again with moist cloth, keep aside for 2 hours to allow the dough to rise.

4 Heat the oven till moderately hot—175 °C (350 °F).

5 Divide the dough into 6 balls and place on a lightly floured surface. Sprinkle onion and melon seeds, flatten the balls slightly, cover and keep aside for 5 minutes.

6 Flatten each ball between the palms to make a round disc, then stretch on one side to form an elongated oval.

7 Place on a greased baking tray and bake for 2-3 min. Serve hot.

NAAN

A delicious Royal Indian bread with a touch of onions & melon seeds

Serves: 4-5

Preparation time: 3 hours

Cooking time: 20 minutes

Stuffed Parantha

Ingredients

Flour 200 gms / 1 cup
Butter 45 gms / 3 tbs
Water 80 ml / ½ cup

For the filling:

Potatoes, boiled, mashed 150 gms / 3/4 cup
Ginger, chopped 20 gms / 4 tsp
Green chillies, chopped 10 gms / 2 tsp
Green coriander, chopped 10 gms / 2 tsp
Salt 5 gms / ½ tsp
Red chilli powder 3 gms / ½ tsp
Pomegranate *(anardana)* seeds 8 gms / 1½ tsp
Oil 45 gms / 3 tbs

Method

1 Mix butter into the flour and knead the flour using water into a smooth pliable dough.

2 For the filling, mix together the potatoes, ginger, green chillies, green coriander, salt, red chilli powder and pomegranate seeds. Divide the filling into 4 equal portions.

3 Divide the dough into 4 equal portions and shape into balls. Flatten each ball between palm and fingers. Place one portion of filling in the centre and seal the edges.

4 Dust with flour and roll out with a rolling pin into a 8" diameter pancake.

5 Heat a tawa (griddle), brush the surface with oil. Place the stuffed parantha on the griddle and cook for a few seconds, brush with oil, turn over and similarly cook on the other side.

6 Both sides of the stuffed parantha should be crisp and delicately browned. Remove and serve immediately, accompanied by any yoghurt preparation.

STUFFED PARANTHA

Spicy Potato filling in a leavened whole wheat bread

Serves: 4

Preparation time: 30 minutes

Cooking time: 20 minutes

Tandoori Roti

Ingredients

Whole wheat flour 1 kg
Salt 20 gms / 4 tsp
Water 700 ml / 3 ½ cups

Method

1 Seive flour and salt in a mixing bowl. Add water and knead into a smooth and elastic dough. Cover with a moist cloth and keep aside for 1 hour.

2 Place the dough on a floured board. Divide into 16 equal portions and shape into balls. Allow to rest for 5 minutes.

3 Flatten between palms moistened with a little water and oil.

4 Place carefully in a tandoor and cook till light brown in colour.

5 Remove from tandoor and serve, as an accompaniment to any curry dish.

TANDOORI ROTI

Unleavened wheat flour pancakes cooked in a tandoor

Serves: 4

Preparation time: 1 hour 15 minutes

Cooking time: 20 minutes

Daal Makhani

Ingredients

Black lentils, whole
(kali urad daal) 300 gms / 1½ cups
Butter 120 gms / ½ cup
Ginger paste (pg. 105) 20 gms / 4 tsp
Garlic paste (pg. 105) 20 gms / 4 tsp
Green chillies, sliced 2
Tomato purée (pg. 105) 160 ml / 3/4 cup
Salt to taste
Chilli powder 5 gms / 1 tsp
Green coriander, chopped 10 gms / 2 tsp
Cream 160 ml / 3/4 cup

Method

1 Soak lentils for at least 3 hrs; best soaked overnight.

2 Cook lentils in water (1½ lts) over low heat till grain splits. Stir to mash them. Keep aside.

3 Heat butter, fry ginger and garlic pastes. Add green chillies, tomato puree, salt and chilli powder. Cook for 2-3 minutes, add the cooked lentils alongwith coriander and cream (leaving 1 tbs aside). Cook further for 10-15 minutes, stirring occasionally.

4 Serve hot, garnished with the reserved cream and accompanied by any Indian bread.

DAAL MAKHANI

Black lentils cooked in cream, over slow fire. A favourite with almost all gourmets

Serves: 4

Preparation time: 6-7 hours

Cooking time: 3 hours

Yellow Daal

Ingredients

Lentils *(arhar daal)* 240 gms / 1 cup
Salt to taste
Yellow chilli powder 5 gms / 1 tsp
Garlic paste (pg. 105) 15 gms / 1 tbs
Cream 120 gms / ½ cup
Yoghurt 240 gms / 1 cup
Butter or clarified butter *(ghee)*
120 gms / ½ cup
Garlic, chopped 15 gms / 1 tbs
Cumin *(jeera)* seeds 3 gms / ½ tsp
Onions, chopped 120 gms / ½ cup
Red chillies, whole 4
Pepper to taste

Method

1 Pick and wash lentils. Boil with (1 litre) water, salt and yellow chilli powder till tender.

2 Add garlic paste and cook for a further 10 minutes.

3 Add the cream and yoghurt and half of butter/clarified butter. Cook again for 10 minutes, stirring frequently so that the butter/clarified butter is incorporated into the daal. Add pepper to taste.

4 Heat remaining half of the butter/clarified butter in a pan. Sauté the chopped garlic, cumin and onions for 2 minutes. Add whole red chillies and sauté till brown. Add to the cooked lentils.

5 Serve hot with a knob of butter.

YELLOW DAAL

A lentil delicacy from the kitchen of the Mughal Kings

Serves: 4

Preparation: 15 minutes

Cooking: 30 minutes

DAAL PANCHMELA

Ingredients

Lentils (malka masoor daal) 45 gms / 3 tbs
Lentils *(chana daal)* 45 gms / 3 tbs
Lentils *(dhuli urad daal)* 45 gms / 3 tbs
Lentils *(arhar daal)* 45 gms / 3 tbs
Lentils *(dhuli moong daal)* 45 gms / 3 tbs
Water as required
Salt 10 gms / 2 tsp
Turmeric *(haldi)* powder 5 gms / 1 tsp
Red chilli powder 5 gms / 1 tsp
Oil 30 ml / 2 tbs
Butter 15 gms / 1 tbs
Cumin *(jeera)* seeds 5 gms / 1 tsp
Ginger, chopped 10 gms / 2 tsp
Tomatoes, chopped 60 gms / 4 tbs
Green coriander, chopped 5 gms / 1 tsp

Method

1 Pick, clean and wash the lentils.

2 Put the lentils alongwith water, salt, turmeric powder and red chilli powder in a *handi* (pot) and cook on low heat for 40-45 minutes till the lentils are tender.

3 Remove from heat and keep aside.

4 Heat oil and butter in a pan, add cumin and sauté till they crackle. Add ginger, stir-fry to a light brown colour.

5 Add the tomatoes and sauté for a minute. Stir in the green coriander and remove from heat.

6 Temper the cooked lentils with this mixture and serve hot, accompanied by any Indian bread.

DAAL PANCHMELA

Mixed lentil curry

Serves: 4

Preparation time: 15 minutes

Cooking time: 1 hour

Gramflour Dumplings in a Tangy Yoghurt Curry

Ingredients

Yoghurt 360 gms / 1½ cups
Salt to taste
Red chilli powder 5 gms / 1 tsp
Green chillies, chopped 5
Turmeric *(haldi)* powder 5 gms / 1 tsp
Gramflour *(besan)* 120 gms / ½ cup
Soda bi-carb a pinch
Oil to deep fry
Groundnut oil 60 ml / 4 tbs
Potatoes, cut round 150 gms
Onion rounds (¼" thick) 150 gms
Cumin *(jeera)* seeds 3 gms / ½ tsp
Carom *(ajwain)* seeds 3 gms / ½ tsp
Mustard *(sarson)* seeds 3 gms / ½ tsp
Fenugreek *(methi)* seeds
3 gms / ½ tsp
Red chillies, whole 4

Method

1 Whisk yoghurt, salt, red chilli powder, turmeric and half the gramflour together in a bowl. Keep aside.

2 Sieve the other half of the gram flour and soda bi-carb together, add the carom seeds and mix enough water to make a thick batter. Beat well. Add green chillies.

3 Heat enough oil in a kadhai to deep fry. Drop large spoonfuls of the batter in the oil to get 1½ inch puffy dumplings.

4 Fry till golden brown on both sides. Remove and keep aside.

5 Heat 3 tbs groundnut oil in a handi, add the yoghurt mixture and 720 ml/3 cups water. Bring to a boil, reduce to a low heat and simmer for 8-10 minutes, stirring constantly to avoid the yoghurt from curdling.

6 Add the potatoes and onions and cook till potatoes are done.

7 Add the dumplings and simmer for 3 minutes.

8 Heat the remaining groundnut oil in a small frying pan. Add the cumin, mustard, fenugreek and carom seeds. Sauté till they crackle. Add the whole red chillies and stir.

9 Pour this tempering over the simmering hot curry and serve.

GRAMFLOUR DUMPLINGS IN A TANGY YOGHURT CURRY

Serves: 4

Preparation time: 45 minutes

Cooking time: 30 minutes

Tangy Lentil Soup

Ingredients

Lentils *(toor daal)* 100 gms / ½ cup
Turmeric *(haldi)* powder 5 gms / 1 tsp
Green chilli 1
Tomatoes 2-3
Mustard *(raee)* seeds 5 gms / 1 tsp
Whole red chillies 5
Asafoetida 1 gm
Garlic, crushed 30 gms / 2 tbs
Curry leaves 10
Oil 15 ml / 1 tbs
Tamarind (pulp) 100 gms / ½ cup
Peppercorns 3-4

Method

1 Heat oil in a sauce pan. Add mustard seeds and saute until they begin to crackle. Add whole red chillies, curry leaves, asafoetida and crushed garlic, stir for a few seconds.

2 Add turmeric, washed and cleaned toor dal, quarters of tomatoes, pepper corns, deseeded and slit green chillies, tamarind pulp and salt. Stir and add approximately 1 litre of water.

3 Bring to a boil and let it simmer until dal is mashed.

4 Serve hot, as a starter or an accompaniment to a meal.

TANGY LENTIL SOUP

Serves:4

Preparation: 30 minutes

Cooking: 15 minutes

Gulab Jamum

Ingredients

Khoya (pg. 105) 300 gms / 1½ cups
Chenna 60 gms / 4 tbs
Soda bi-carb a pinch
Flour 45 gms / 3 tbs
Sugar 960 gms / ½ cups
Saffron *(kesar)* a few strands
Green cardamoms *(choti elaichi)*, pealed 5
Rosewater 2 drops
Clarified butter *(ghee)* to deep fry

Method

1 Knead khoya and chenna gently together.

2 Dissolve soda bi-carb in (1tsp) teaspoon water.

3 Add flour and soda to the khoya and chenna mixure. Knead to a smooth, soft, dough-like consistency.

4 Make 24 balls and smoothen by rolling between your palms.

5 Boil sugar in (500 gms) 2½ cups water for 5-7 minutes till the syrup turns golden brown.

6 **For the filling,** pound saffron and mix with green cardamom seeds and rosewater.

7 Flatten balls. Place a pinch of the filling in the centre, seal and roll into balls again.

8 Heat clarified butter *(ghee)* in a wok *(kadhai)* and slide the balls a few at a time. Gently shake the pan till the balls rise to the surface.

9 Remove with slotted spoon and immediately immerse in syrup.

10 Remove to a bowl alongwith sugar syrup and serve hot.

Gulab Jamum

Deep fried chenna dumplings in sugar syrup

Serves: 4

Preparation time: 30 minutes

Cooking time: 1 hour

RAS MALAI

Ingredients

For the flavoured milk:
Whole milk 1 litre / 5 cups
Cream 240 ml / 1⅓ cup
Sugar 60 gms / 4 tbs
Green cardamom *(choti elaichi)* seeds, crushed 5 gms / 1 tsp

For the filling:
Saffron threads a pinch
Cream 20 ml / 4 tsp
Pistachios, blanched, minced 15 gms/1 tbs
Golden raisens, minced 15 gms / 1 tbs
Almonds, blanched, minced 15 gms / 1tbs
Honey 7 ml / 1½ tsp

For the medallions:
Whole milk 2 liters / 10 cups
Lemon juice, strained 60 ml / 4 tbs
Water 1.5 liters/ 7 cups
Sugar 1 kg / 5 cups
Cornstarch (dissolved) 30 gms/2 tbs

Method

1 **For the flavoured milk,** boil milk in a pan till it reduces to a cup. Add cream, sugar, cardamom, boil for 5 minutes and pour to a shallow dish.

2 **For the filling,** powder the saffron threads and mix with cream, nuts, raisins and honey. Divide into 16 portions.

3 **For the medallions,** boil milk in a pan, add lemon juice to curdle the milk and cheese to seperate from whey. Remove from heat and keep aside.

4 Pour the cheese mixture into a cheese cloth and rinse under running water for 10 minutes. Squeeze and drain excess water.

5 Prepare sugar syrup by boiling water and sugar. Remove and keep aside.

6 Unwrap cheese on a clean work surface and crumble. Divide into 16 portions. Place 1 portion of filling in each portion of cheese and shape into medallion.

7 Reheat sugar syrup and slide the prepared medallions. Increase heat and boil for 20 minutes adding constantly with ¼ cup water after every 4 minutes to maintain the consistency of syrup.

8 Gently lift the medallion with a slotted spoon and slip into the flavoured milk. Garnish with vetivier and serve chilled.

RAS MALAI

Sweet medallions in saffron flavoured milk

Serves: 8

Preparation time: 1 hour

Cooking time: 1 hour 30 minutes

Rasgoola

Ingredients

Whole milk 2 lts / 10 cups
Lemon juice 60 ml / 4 tbs
Water 2 lts / 8 cups
Sugar 1.5 kg
Cornstarch (dissolved in 2 tbs water)
15 gms / 1 tbs
Vetivier *(kewda)* essence
3 gms / ½ tsp

Method

1 Take milk in a heavy bottomed pan, bring to a frothing boil, reduce heat. Add lemon juice to curdle milk. Remove from heat and keep aside for 10 minutes.

2 Pour the cheese-whey mixture into a moist cheese cloth, gather the four corners of the cloth and rinse it under tap water for about 10 minutes. Gently twist the cloth to squeeze out excess water. Tie up the corners and hang for 20 minutes to allow all excess water to drain.

3 Meanwhile boil sugar and water in a pan until sugar dissolves completely. Cook on high heat for 3-4 minutes, remove from heat and keep aside.

4 Unwrap the cheese on a clear work surface and crumble it repeatedly till it becomes fluffy and smooth.

5 Collect all the cheese into one big portion and coat with a thin layer of oil from all sides. Divide into 16 portions and shape each into a smooth ball.

6 Reheat the sugar syrup, bring to a boil and slide in the prepared balls. Increase heat and boil continuously for about 20 minutes adding cornstarch with ¼ cup water after 4 minutes of boiling. Thereafter ¼ cup of water to maintain the consistency of syrup. Take care to add the water directly into the syrup and not on the balls. Remove from heat.

7 Allow to cool for 10 minutes, sprinkle the vetivier essence. Leave the rasgoolas to soak at room temperature for atleast 4 hours. Serve chilled or at room temperature alongwith syrup.

RASGOOLA

Chenna dumplings in syrup

Serves: 8

Preparation time: 2 hours

Cooking time: 50 minutes

Rajbhog

Ingredients

For the filling:
Whole milk 320 ml, Sugar 30 gms / 2 tbs
Pistachios, grated 45 gms / 3 tbs
Green cardamoms *(choti elaichi)*, crushed 5

For the chenna dumplings:
Whole milk 2 litres
Lemon juice, strained 60 ml / 4 tbs
Water 2 litres / 10 cups,
Sugar 1.5 kg / 7½ cups
Cornstarch (dissolved in 2tbs water) 15 gms /1tbs
Rose essence ½ tsp

Method

1 **For the filling**, boil milk and sugar in a pan, till reduces to half. Add nuts, cardamom, cook until the mixture leaves the sides of the pan. Scrape into a paste and keep aside to cool.

2 **For the chenna dumplings,** heat milk over high heat, bring to a boil. Reduce heat and add lemon juice to curdle the milk. Remove and keep aside.

3 Pour the cheese whey mixture into a moist cheese cloth. Gather r corners of the cloth and rinse under tap water. Squeeze out excess water by gently twisting the cloth.

4 Boil sugar and water in a pan until sugar completely dissolves. Remove from heat and keep aside.

5 Unwrap cheese on a clean work surface and crumble it. Divide into 8 balls and flatten. Divide filling equally and place one in the centre of patty and roll into ball.

6 Heat sugar syrup, slide in prepared balls. Boil for 20 minutes adding cornstarch with ¼ cup water to maintain the consistency of syrup.

7 Remove and allow to cool. Sprinkle rose essence and serve chilled or at room temperature.

RAJBHOG

Chenna dumplings stuffed with cardamoms, dipped in sugar syrup

Serves: 8

Preparation time: 30 minutes

Cooking time: 3-4 hours

Chenna Payas

Ingredients

Milk 2 ½ litres / 12 ½ cups
Or Chenna 350 gms / 1¾ cups
Sugar 400 gms / 2 cups
Water 300 ml / 1½ cup
Refined flour *(maida)* 25 gms / 5 tsp
Milk 1 litre / 5 cups
Sugar 60 gms / 4 tbs
Green cardamom *(choti elaichi)* powder 3 gms / ½ tsp
Saffron *(kesar)* 2 gms / ⅓ tsp
Almond, slivered 10 gms / 2 tsp
Pistachios, slivered 10 gms / 2 tsp
Saffron *(kesar)* a few strands

Method

1 Boil milk in a pan and curdle it by adding white vinegar or lemon juice.

2 Boil sugar and water for the sugar syrup. Reduce heat to low. Drain the whey and mash the curd cheese well. Seperate 300 gms for payas and 50 gms for the dumplings.

3 **For the dumplings,** make 40 dumplings and simmer in sugar syrup till they swell upto double their size. (To aid in swelling, the simmering syrup should be allowed to froth, by adding refined flour *(maida)* before adding the dumplings). Remove from the sugar syrup and keep aside.

4 **For the payas,** cook the curd cheese seperated for the payas in a wok *(kadhai)* on very low heat. Add sugar and stir continuously. Cook till it begins to leave the sides. Remove from heat and allow to cool.

5 **For the rabari,** cook milk in a wok *(kadhai)*, till it reduces to ⅓, add the cardamom powder and saffron. Remove from heat and stir in sugar.

6 Transfer rabari to the wok *(kadhai)* containing the payas and cook for about 10-12 minutes. Remove from heat and allow to cool.

7 Gently fold in the prepared 'rasgoolas' dumplings into the prepared payas and serve chilled, garnished with almonds, pistachios and saffron.

CHENNA PAYAS

Small dumplings of curdled milk in flavoured rabari, one of the best Indian sweets

Serves: 4

Preparation time: 20 minutes

Cooking time: 45 minutes

LAVANG LATIKA

Ingredients

Refined flour 200 gms / 1 cup
Saffron *(kesar)* a few strands soaked with in 1 tbs water
Water 60 ml / 4 tbs
Veg.oil 30 ml / 2 tbs

For the filling:

Khoya, mashed (pg. 105) 125 gms / 3/4 cup
Almonds, slivered 20 gms / 4 tsp
Pistachios, slivered 20 gms / 4 tsp
Clove *(laung)* powder 3 gms / ½ tsp
Sugar, powdered 30 gms / 2 tbs
Cloves *(laung)* 12
Oil for frying

For the sugar syrup:

Sugar 500 gms / 2 ½ cups
Water 700 ml / 3 ½ cups

Method

1 Sieve the flour and make a well in the centre.

2 Add saffron and vegetable oil. Mix well. Add water knead to make a hard dough. Cover with a wet cloth and allow to rest for 15 minutes.

3 **For the filling,** mix together khoya, almonds, pistachios, clove powder and sugar. Divide into 12 equal portions.

4 Boil sugar with water to prepare the sugar syrup.

5 Divide the dough into 12 equal portions and shape into balls. Roll out each ball into 6" diameter pancakes.

6 Place one portion of filling in the centre of each pancake and brush the edges with water. Fold the pancakes from the right edge to the centre and press firmly to seal in the filling. Repeat from left edge to give a 2" wide strip.

7 Keeping the folded side out, make a ring with the strip. Brush the edges with water and press firmly to seal, secure with a clove.

8 Shallow fry on very low heat till crisp and golden brown in colour. Remove and drain excess oil.

9 Dip in hot sugar syrup to submerge completely, turning gently if required. Allow to soak for 2-3 minutes. Remove and serve.

LAVANG LATIKA

Clove flavoured stuffed and rolled pancakes, deep fried and seized in syrup

Serves: 4

Preparation time: 1 hour

Cooking time: 30 minutes

Imarti

Ingredients

Lentils *(dhuli urad daal)*
250 gms / 1¼ cups
Water 500 ml / 2½ cups
Refined flour *(maida)* 25 gms / 5 tsp
Cornflour 25 gms / 5 tsp
Yellow colour 5 ml / 1 tsp
Clarified butter *(ghee)* 750 ml / 3 ¾ cups

For the sugar syrup:

Sugar 1 kg 250 gms / 6 1/4 cups
Water 1½ litre / 7 cups
Saffron *(kesar)* a few strands
Vetivier *(kewda)* water 5 ml / 1 tsp

Method

1 Wash and soak the lentils in water for 1 hour.

2 Drain the lentils and blend to a coarse paste 'peethi'. Add colour and keep aside.

3 Prepare the sugar syrup by boiling water alongwith sugar for about 20 minutes till it reaches a thread-like consistency. Stir in the saffron and vetivier. Reduce heat to low.

4 Heat the clarified butter in a flat wok *(kadhai)* wok.

5 Stuff the prepared paste into a cloth piping bag and pipe out the paste in the kadhai in circles and then overlapping with circles on the borders.

6 Fry for 2-3 minutes on each side until a golden yellow colour is achieved.

7 Remove and immerse directly into the hot sugar syrup. Allow to soak for for 2 minutes.

8 Remove, drain excess syrup and serve hot.

IMARTI

Lentil roundels seized in saffron flavoured sugar syrup

Serves: 4

Preparation time: 1 hour 15 minutes

Cooking time: 30-40 minutes

Malpua

Ingredients

Toned milk 2 litres / 10 cups
Khoya, grated (pg. 105) 60 gms / 4 tbs
Flour 20 gms / 4 tsp
Cornflour 25 gms / 5 tsp
Green cardamom *(choti elaichi)* powder 3 gms / ½ tsp

For the sugar syrup:

Water 250 gms / 1 ⅓ cups
Sugar 500 gms / 2 ½ cups
Vetivier *(kewda)* essence 5 ml / 1 tsp
Yellow colour 3 gms / ½ tsp
Clarified butter *(ghee)* for frying

For garnishing:

Pistachios, chopped, blanched 20 gms / 4 tsp
Saffron *(kesar)* a few strands

Method

1 Boil milk in a kadhai (wok) till it reduces to ¼.

2 Add khoya and reduce heat to low, stir continuously till the khoya is completely dissolved.

3 Remove from heat onto a mixing bowl and allow to cool. Add flour, cornflour, green cardamom powder and mix thoroughly to make a batter.

4 In a pan, boil water alongwith sugar and cook till it reaches a thread like consistency. Mix in vetivier and yellow colour.

5 Heat clarified butter (ghee) in a frying pan. Add one ladle of batter and fry on both sides till golden brown in colour. Remove, drain excess oil and immerse directly into the sugar syrup. Repeat the same process until all the batter is used up.

6 Allow the malpua's to soak in syrup for a few minutes.

7 Remove from the sugar syrup and fold the malpua's into half or triangles. Arrange neatly on a serving platter and serve hot, garnished with pistachios and saffron and accompanied by Rabari (page 88).

MALPUA

Shallow fried pancakes, soaked in saffron flavoured sugar syrup

Serves: 4

Preparation time: 45 minutes

Cooking time: 20 minutes

Shahi Tukda Nawabi

Ingredients

Milk 1 litre / 5 cups
Green cardamom *(choti elaichi)* powder 3 gms / 1/3 tsp
Saffron *(kesar)* a few strands
Sugar 100 gms / ½ cup
Milk bread slices 8
Clarified butter *(ghee)* 200 gms / 1 cup

For the rabari

Milk 2 litres / 10 cups
Sugar 100 gms / ½ cup
Green cardamom *(choti elaichi)* powder 3 gms / ½ tsp
Saffron *(kesar)* a few strands
Almonds, slivered 10 gms / 2 tsp
Pistachios, slivered 10 gms / 2 tsp
Saffron *(kesar)* a few strands

Method

1 Heat milk in a thick bottomed pan and bring to a boil. Add the cardamom powder and saffron. Remove from heat and mix in the sugar. Keep aside.

2 Heat clarified butter *(ghee)* in a seperate pan and fry the bread slices lightly. Remove, drain excess clarified butter.

3 Dip the fried bread slices in the prepared milk to immerse completely. Allow to stand for 10-15 minutes.

4 **For the rabari:** Heat milk in a pan and cook till it reduces to 1/3. Stir in the sugar, cardamom powder and saffron. Remove from heat and keep aside to cool.

5 Carefully lift the bread slices from the milk and place on a serving platter. Pour the rabari on top, garnish with slivered almonds and pistachios and strands of saffron.

6 Serve chilled or at room temperature.

SHAHI TUKDA NAWABI

A royal dessert of slices of rich bread soaked in a thickened flavoured milk

Serves: 4

Preparation time: 15 minutes

Cooking time: 1 hour

BESAN LADOO

Ingredients

Gramflour *(besan)*, sifted
200 gms / 2 cups
Butter (unsalted) / Oil 180 ml / ¾ cup
Coconut, dried and grated 30 gms / 2 tbs
Walnuts, chopped 30 gms / 2 tbs
Nutmeg *(jaiphal)*, ground a pinch
Sugar 110 gms / ½ cup

Method

1 Melt butter/oil in a heavy bottomed pan over moderately low heat. Add gramflour, coconut, walnuts and nutmeg, cook, for about 5 minutes stirring constantly. Add sugar and continue to cook for 10-15 minutes or until the mixture is thick and deep golden brown.

2 Turn onto a clean flat surface, when cool enough to handle, shape into 24 equal sized balls.

3 Garnish with slivered nuts and serve at room temperature. Can be stored upto 10-15 days.

BESAN LADOO

Sweet gramflour balls with coconut and walnuts

Makes: 2 dozen balls

Preparation time:10 minutes

Cooking time: 20 minutes

KESAR SANDESH

Ingredients

Saffron *(kesar)* 3 gms / ½ tsp
Whole milk 320 ml / 1½ cups
Lemon juice 60 ml / 4 tbs
Sugar, powdered 110 gms / ½ cups

Method

1 Roast saffron in a dry pan and pound to a fine powder. Dissolve in hot milk (2 tbs) and keep aside.

2 Heat milk in a pan over high heat, bring to a frothing boil, stirring continuously. Reduce heat, add lemon juice to make the milk curdle and the cheese to separate from the whey. If it does not, then add another tbs of lemon juice. Remove from heat and set aside to cool.

3 Pour the cheese-whey mixture into a moist cheese cloth, gather the 4 corners of the cloth and rinse under tap water for 10 minutes. Gently twist the cloth to squeeze out excess water. Tie up the corners and hang for 20-30 minutes to allow all excess water to drain.

4 Unwrap the cheese on a clean work surfacc and crumblc repeatedly till it becomes fluffy and even. Blend in the powdered sugar and knead till it becomes smooth and grainless.

5 Transfer cheese-sugar (*chenna*) mixture to a heavy bottomed pan, cook for 10-15 minutes until mixture becomes a little thickened and glossy.

6 Divide the mixture into two portions. Mix in the dissolved saffron into one portion till it is thorougly mixed and turns yellow. Divide the yellow *chenna* mixture into 2 portions again.

7 Spread three alternate layers of yellow, white and yellow *chenna* on a buttered tray to form a 1½" - 2" thick cake. Allow to cool and cut into 1½" thick squares and serve at room temperature or slightly cooled.

KESAR SANDESH

Saffron cheese fudge

Serves: 4

Preparation time: 1 hour 30 minutes

Cooking time: 1 hour

Coconut Burfee

Ingredients

Coconut powder 600 gms / 3 cups
Green cardamom *(choti elaichi)* powder 5 gms / 1 tsp
Pistachios / Silver leaf for garnishing
Saffron *(kesar)* a few strands
Sugar 60 gms / 4 tbs
Sweet ittar 1 drop
Water 80 ml / 1/3 cup

Method

1. Put sugar and water to heat in a pan. Stir continuously till the sugar is completely dissolved.
2. Bring to boil. Add coconut powder, sweet ittar, saffron and green cardamom powder. Mix well.
3. Remove from heat and spread evenly on a greased baking tray. Cool and cut into 8 pieces.
4. Garnish with pistachios or silver leaf

Coconut Burfee

Coconut fudge, famous all over India

Serves: 4

Preparation time: 10 minutes

Cooking time: 10 minutes

Gajrela

Ingredients

Carrots, finely grated 1 kg
Almonds 100 gms / ½ cup
Clarified butter *(ghee)* 60 ml / 4 tbs
Green cardamoms *(choti elaichi)* 10
Milk, full cream 1 litre / 5 cups
Pistachios 50 gms / ¼ cup
Sugar 180 gms / 1 scant cup

Method

1 In a heavy pan bring the milk to a slow boil, stirring with a wooden spoon.

2 Add the grated carrots and green cardamoms and cook over medium heat for 30-45 minutes or until the milk is almost evaporated.

3 Add the sugar, stir and cook until the sugar is completely dissolved.

4 Add the ghee, stir and cook until the carrots are slightly caramelized.

5 Reduce the heat, add the almonds and pistachios, and cook for 3-4 minutes.

6 Serve hot. Garnish with pistachio/almond flakes and grated khoya (page 105).

GAJRELA

Grated carrots cooked in thickened milk, garnished with nuts and raisins

Serves: 4-5

Preparation time: 10 minutes

Cooking time: 1 hour

Moong Daal Halwa

Ingredients

Lentils *(moong daal)* 120 gms / ½ cup
Green cardamoms *(choti elaichi)* 2
Cashewnuts, broken 10 gms / 2 tsp
Clarified butter *(ghee)* 30 gms / 2 tbs
Khoya, fresh, grated (pg. 105)
60 gms / ¼ cup
Pistachios, chopped 10
Sugar 60 gms / 4 tbs
Water 120 ml / ½ cup

Method

1 Wash and soak the lentils for 30 minutes. Drain out water and grind into a rough paste.

2 Heat ghee in a kadhai and fry the lentil paste till light golden in colour.

3 Put the sugar and water to boil in another pan. Stir continuously till the sugar dissolves completely. Boil rapidly for 5 minutes. Add to the fried daal.

4 Cook, stirring vigorously till the mixture becomes thick. Add green cardamom powder.

5 Garnish with khoya, cashewnuts and pistachios. Serve hot.

MOONG DAAL HALWA

Ground and fried lentils are turned into a delicious sweet dish

Serves: 4

Preparation time: 40 minutes

Cooking time: 20 minutes

Kheer

Ingredients

Milk 1 litre / 4¼ cups
Rice, long grain 60 gms / ¼ cup
Almonds 15 gms / 1 tbs
Cardamom powder 5 gms / 1 tsp
Clarified butter *(ghee)* 10 ml / 2 tsp
Milk to dissolve saffron 30 ml / 2 tbs
Raisins 10 gms / 2 tsp
Saffron *(kesar)* a few strands
Sugar 120 gms / ½ cup

Method

1 Wash and soak rice for an hour.

2 Blanch almonds. Cut into slivers.

3 Dissolve the saffron in warm milk and keep aside.

4 Boil milk in a *handi* (pot).

5 In another *handi* (pot) heat the clarified butter, add rice andstir fry for 4-5 minutes till it begins to brown lightly.

6 Add the milk and bring to boil, stirring constantly to prevent rice from sticking. Simmer till rice is cooked.

7 Stir in the sugar. Simmer till milk thickens.

8 Stir in cardamom powder, raisins and almonds.

9 Sprinkle saffron and serve hot in winter and cold in summer.

KHEER

A rich and creamy rice pudding

Serves: 4

Preparation time: 1 hour

Cooking time: 1 hour 30 minutes

Mango Kulfi

Ingredients

Mango pulp 450 ml / 2¼ cups
Milk 1 litre / 5 cups
Sugar 45 gms / 3 tbs
Saffron *(kesar)* a few strands
Cream (heavy) 150 ml / ¾ cups

Method

1 Boil milk into a heavy bottomed pan, lower heat, let it simmer, add sugar, cook till quantity is reduced to a third and it is thick and creamy.

2 Add mango pulp and saffron, cook further for 2 minutes, cool to room temperature and mix in the cream.

3 Spoon the mixture into 6-8 moulds. Cover tightly with foil and freeze for at least 6 hours. Shake the mould thrice during first hour of freezing.

4 Remove from refrigerator, dip the bottom of the mould in hot water and invert onto a dish. Serve immediately.

MANGO KULFI

Home made mango ice cream

Serves: 4-6

Preparation time: 20 minutes

Cooking time: 30 minutes + 8 hours for setting

KULFI

Ingredients

Milk 1½ litres / 7 cups
Saffron *(kesar)* a few strands
Yellow colour 2-3 drops
Sugar 100 gms / ½ cup
Green cardamom *(choti elaichi)* powder a pinch
Pistachios, blanched 20 gms / 4 tsp
Cashewnuts, chopped 20 gms / 4 tsp

Method

1 Soak saffron in 1 tbs water.

2 Heat milk in a *kadhai* (wok), add yellow colour, cook on medium heat stirring constantly for about 20 minutes till it reduces to ¼ th. Remove milk from heat and stir in sugar till completely dissolved.

3 Add the remaining ingredients, mix well and pour the mixture into kulfi moulds.

4 Keep the moulds in a freezer for 1½ hours to allow to set.

5 Remove from the freezer, dip the bottom of the moulds in hot water for a few seconds. Invert onto a serving plate and serve immediately, accompanied by Falooda.

FALOODA

Ingredients

Water 400 ml / 2 cups
Cornflour 100 gms / ½ cup
Yellow colour (optional) a few drops

Method

1 Take water in a *kadhai* (wok), add the cornflour and mix well. Stir in the yellow colour.

2 Cook on low heat stirring continuously till the mixture thickens and becomes gelatinous. Remove from heat and pour into a falooda press.

3 Press the mixture out in one continous stream without stopping into a container of cold water.

4 Change the cold water and store the falooda in a refrigerator and use as required.

5 If desired falooda can be flavoured with Roohafza/ Vetivier/Rose water. Serve chilled, as an accompaniment to Kulfi.

KULFI

Rich and flavourful home made ice cream

Serves: 4

Preparation time: 2 hours

Cooking time: 30 minutes

FALOODA

Freshly prepared cornflour vermicelli served with Kulfi

Serves: 4

Preparation time: 10 minutes

Cooking time: 15-20 minutes

Kujja Kulfi

Ingredients

Milk 1 litre / 5 cups
Saffron *(kesar)* a few strands
Sugar 60 gms / 4 tsp
Yellow colour 2-3 drops
Green cardamom *(choti elaichi)* powder a pinch
Cashewnuts, chopped 20 gms / 4 tsp
Pistachios, blanched, chopped 15 gms / 1 tbs

Method

1 Soak the saffron in 1 tbs water.

2 Heat milk in a *kadhai* (wok) and cook on medium heat for about 20 minutcs, stirring constantly till reduced to ¼ th.

3 Remove milk from heat and stir in the sugar till it is completely dissolved.

4 Mix in the soaked saffron, yellow colour, green cardamom powder and the nuts.

5 Fill into earthenware moulds 'kujja', cover with a lid and seal with dough.

6 Place the moulds in a freezer for 1½ hours to allow to set.

7 Remove from the freezer, remove the lid and serve immediately.

KUJJA KULFI

This home made ice cream is set and served in special earthenware cups

Serves: 4

Preparation time: 2 hours

Cooking time: 30 minutes

Khasta Roti

Ingredients

Whole wheat flour 500 gms / 2½ cups
Carom *(ajwain)* seeds 15 gms / 1 tbs
Salt to taste
Sugar 12 gms / 2½ tsp
Water 300 ml / 1½ cups

Method

1 To the sieved flour, add salt, sugar and carom seeds. Knead into a hard dough with water. Cover with a moist cloth and keep aside for 15 minutes.

2 Divide the dough into 10 equal portions and roll into balls. Dust and roll into 10 cm rotis. Prick with a fork evenly.

3 Bake the rotis for 8-10 minutes in an oven at 175 °C (350 °F) or till light brown in colour.

4 Serve hot, as an accompaniment to any curry dish.

KHASTA ROTI

Whole wheat oven baked bread

Serves: 4-5

Preparation time: 25 minutes

Cooking time: 10-15 minutes

RABARI

Ingredients

Milk 1½ litres / 7 cups
Khoya, grated (pg. 105) 100 gms / ½ cup
Sugar 100 gms / ½ cup
Green cardamom *(choti elaichi)* powder a pinch
Saffron *(kesar)* a few strands
Pistachios, blanched, chopped 20 gms / 4 tsp
Vetivier *(kewda)* water 3-4 drops

Method

1 Heat milk in a *kadhai* (wok), on moderate heat. Stir continuously till the milk reduces to 1/5th.

2 Add khoya and cook on very low heat for 2-3 minutes, stirring continuously till the khoya is dissolved.

3 Add the sugar and cardamom powder and stir till sugar is completely dissolved.

4 Remove from heat and transfer to a serving dish. Allow to cool and refrigerate.

5 Garnish with saffron, pictachios and vetivier and serve.

Rabari

Vetivier and saffron flavoured thickened milk

Serves: 4

Preparation time: 10 minutes

Cooking time: 35 minutes

Makhana ki Kheer

Ingredients

Phool makhana (popped lotus seeds) 60 gms / 4 tbs
Oil for frying
Milk 1½ litres / 7 cups
Raisins 20 gms / 4 tsp
Green cardamom *(choti elaichi)* powder a pinch
Mace *(javitri)* powder a pinch
Nutmeg *(jaiphal)* powder a pinch
Sugar 100 gms / ½ cup
Pistachios, slivered 7 gms / 1½ tsp
Almonds, blanched, slivered 7 gms / 1½ tsp
Cashewnuts, slivered 7 gms / 1½ tsp

Method

1 Clean the popped lotus seeds 'makhanas' and keep aside.

2 Heat oil in a *kadhai* (wok) and deep fry the makhanas on medium heat till crisp and golden brown. Remove from heat and drain excess oil.

3 Crush the fried makhanas with a rolling pin.

4 Heat milk in a seperate *kadhai* (wok) and bring to a boil. Stir in the crushed makhanas, raisins, green cardamom powder, mace powder and nutmeg powder.

5 Reduce heat and cook for about 20 minutes, stirring constantly till the milk reduces to $^{3}/_{4}$th.

6 Stir in the sugar. Remove from heat and transfer to a serving bowl.

7 Serve hot, garnished with slivered pistachios, almonds and cashewnuts.

Makhana ki Kheer

Popped lotus seeds cooked in simmering milk, flavoured with saffron

Serves: 4

Preparation time: 15 minutes

Cooking time: 40 minutes

Dahi Bhalla

Ingredients

For the bhallas:

Lentils *(dhuli urad daal)* 200 gms / 1 cup
Water 600 ml / 3 cups
Salt 3 gms / ½ tsp
Cumin *(jeera)* seeds 5 gms / 1 tsp
Ginger, chopped 10 gms / 2 tsp
Green chillies, chopped 5 gms
Oil 250 ml / 1 1/3 cup

For the yoghurt mixture:

Yoghurt, thick, whisked 400 gms / 2 cups
Sugar 5 gms /1 tsp
Salt 3 gms / ½ tsp
Cumin *(jeera)* seeds, roasted, pounded 4 gms / 3/4 tsp
Black rock salt *(kala namak)* 3 gms / ½ tsp
White pepper powder 3 gms / ½ tsp

For garnishing:

Ginger, julienned 5 gms / 1 tsp
Green chillies, julienned 5 gms / 1 tsp
Green coriander, chopped 5 gms / 1 tsp
Red chilli powder a pinch
Cumin *(jeera)* seeds, roasted, pounded a pinch
Mint leaves 4 sprigs
Tamarind *(Saunth)* chutney (pg. 102) 45 gms / 3 tbs

Method

1 Clean lentils and soak in water for 2 hours. Drain and grind to a fine paste. Add water if required. Remove onto a mixing bowl and add salt, cumin seeds, ginger, green chillies and mix well. Shape into even sized balls.

2 Heat oil in a *kadhai* (wok), add the prepared balls, a few at a time and deep fry till golden brown in colour. (Make a hole in the centre of the ball with the thumb just before frying). Remove, drain on paper towels.

3 Soak prepared bhallas in sufficient luke warm water till they are soft. To yoghurt add all the ingredientsand mix well.

4 Remove bhallas from water, squeeze out excess water and add to the yoghurt. Keep aside for 10-15 minutes.

5 Serve chilled, garnished with ginger, green chillies, green coriander, red chilli powder, cumin powder, mint leaves and tamarind chutney.

DAHI BHALLA

Lentil dumplings in a tangy and spiced yoghurt, served with tamarind chutney

Serves: 4

Preparation time: 2 hours

Cooking time: 30 minutes

Mixed Vegetable Raita

Ingredients

Yoghurt 600 gm / 3 cups
Cumin *(jeera)* seeds 5 gms / 1 tsp
Coriander seeds 5 gms / 1 tsp
Black peppercorns 3 gms / ½ tsp
Salt to taste
Cucumber, chopped 30 gms / 2 tbs
Green chilli, finely chopped 5 gms / 1 tsp
Mint, chopped 5 gms / 1 tsp
Onions, chopped 30 gms / 2 tbs
Tomatoes, chopped 30 gms / 2 tbs
Red chilli powder a pinch

Method

1 Heat a *tawa* (griddle) and broil cumin, coriander seeds and pepper till dark and aromatic.

2 Pound and keep aside.

3 Whisk yoghurt with salt. Add and mix all chopped vegetables.

4 Sprinkle red chilli powder and refrigerate for ½ hour.

5 Serve, as an accompaniment to any curry dish and rice.

Mint Raita

Ingredients

Yoghurt 600 ml / 3 cups
Mint leaves, dried, crushed 75 gms / 5 tbs
Cumin *(jeera)* powder 3 gms / ½ tsp

Method

1 In a bowl, whisk yoghurt alongwith salt and cumin powder.

2 Add the mint leaves.

3 Refrigerate for half an hour.

4 Sprinkle mint leaves (1 tbs) and serve as an accompaniment to any dish.

Mint Raita

Serves: 4

Preparation time: 10 minutes

Boondi Raita

Ingredients

Gramflour *(besan)* 45 gms / 3 tbs
Salt to taste
Baking powder 3 gms / ½ tsp
Water as required
Oil for frying
Yoghurt, thick 925 gms / 4½ cups
Cumin *(jeera)* seeds, roasted, crushed a pinch
Red chilli powder 3 gms / ½ tsp

Method

1 **For the Boondi,** Mix together the gramflour, salt (¼ tsp) and baking powder in a bowl, gradually add water and whisk to a smooth batter, having consistancy of heavy cream.

2 Heat oil in a deep-frying pan. Pour about 2 tbs of batter at a time into a frying spoon with several holes. Hold the spoon above the pan and press the batter through the holes with your fingers. They will froth in the hot oil, then rise to the surface.

3 Fry until crisp and golden in colour. Remove on paper towels to drain. Repeat the process for all the batter.

4 In a bowl of warm water, put 2-3 tbs of boondis, leave to soften, then gently squeeze between palms to remove excess water, keep aside.

5 Whisk yoghurt alongwith salt to taste, cumin seeds, red chilli powder in a bowl until smooth and creamy.

6 Stir in the soaked boondi and serve at room temperature or chilled, as an accompaniment to any meal.

BOONDI RAITA

Serves: 4

Preparation time:
30-40 minutes

ORANGE RAITA

Ingredients

Yoghurt, thick 925 gms / 4½ cups
Salt to taste
Oranges 200 gms /1 cup
Cumin *(jeera)* seeds, roasted, pounded a pinch

Method

1 Whisk yoghurt and salt together.

2 Peel, clean and seperate the oranges into segments, cut into 10 mm squares and add to the yoghurt.

3 Chill and serve, garnished with cumin powder.

WALNUT RAITA

Ingredients

Cucumber 450 gms
Yoghurt, whisked 800 gms / 4 cups
Honey 75 gms / 5 tbs
Raisins, chopped 45 gms / 3 tbs
White pepper powder 3 gms / ½ tsp
Salt to taste
Cumin *(jeera)* seeds, roasted, powdered 3 gms / ½ tsp
Green Coriander, chopped 5 gms / 1 tsp
Walnuts for garnishing

Method

1 Peel and chop the cucumbers finely.

2 To the whisked yoghurt add honey, raisins, cucumber, white pepper powder and salt. Mix well.

3 Transfer to a serving bowl and sprinkle cumin powder. Garnish with green coriander and walnuts.

4 Serve chilled or at room temperature, as an accompaniment to a meal.

Orange Raita

Serves: 4

Preparation time: 15 minutes

Walnut Raita

Serves: 4

Preparation time: 15 minutes

Coconut Chutney

Ingredients

Coconut, shelled, grated 320 gms / 1½ cups
Green chillies, chopped 12 gms / 2½ tsp
Ginger, peeled, chopped 12 gms / 2½ tsp
Lentils *(chana daal)*, roasted 40 gms
Water 200 ml / 1 cup, Salt to taste, Lemon ½

For the tempering:

Oil 10 ml / 2 tsp
Lentils *(urad daal)*, washed 5 gms /1 tsp
Mustard *(raee)* seeds 3 gms / ½ tsp
Red chillies, whole 2

Method

1 Blend green chillies, ginger, coconut, lentil and water into a smooth paste. Add salt and lemon juice.

2 Heat oil in a pan, add the lentils, mustard seeds and red chillies, sauté till they crackle. Pour over chutney and serve cold.

Tomato Chutney

Ingredients

Tomatoes 335 gms / 1¾ cup
Ginger, chopped 8 gms / 1½ tsp
Red chilli powder 3 gms / ½ tsp
Coconut, shelled 28 gms / 5 tsp
Oil 10 gms / 2 tsp
Lentils *(urad daal)*, washed 5 gms /1 tsp
Red chillies, whole 1
Mustard *(raee)* seeds 3 gms / ½ tsp

Method

1 Blanch the tomatoes. Remove and cool.

2 Blend the tomatoes, ginger, red chilli powder and coconut to make a purée.

3 Heat oil in a pan, add the lentils, red chillies and mustard seeds, sauté till they crackle.

4 Pour over the chutney and serve.

COCONUT CHUTNEY

Serves: 4

Preparation time: 15 minutes

TOMATO CHUTNEY

Serves: 4

Preparation time: 10 minutes

Cooking time: 5 minutes

Mint Chutney

Ingredients

Mint, chopped 100 gms / ½ cup
Green coriander, chopped 100 gms / ½ cup
Cumin *(jeera)* seeds 5 gms / 1 tsp
Ginger, finely chopped 25 gms / 5 tsp
Green chillies, chopped 25 gms / 5 tsp
Water 20 ml / 4 tsp
Yoghurt 60 gms / 4 tbs
Dry pomegranate *(anardana)* powder 30 gms / 2 tbs
Salt to taste, Lemon 1

Method

1 Blend the mint leaves and green coriander alongwith all the other ingredients except salt and lemon.

2 Transfer to a serving bowl and mix in salt to taste and juice of a lemon.

Yellow Chutney

Ingredients

Black gram *(chana)* 200 gms / 1 cup
Water 100 ml / ½ cup
Salt to taste, Oil 10 ml / 2 tsp
Mustard *(raee)* seeds 3 gms / ½ tsp
Curry leaves 1 sprig
Red chillies, whole 5

Method

1 Blend black gram with water into a smooth paste, add salt and mix well.

2 Heat oil in a pan, add mustard seeds and sauté till they crackle. Add curry leaves and red chillies. Stir and remove from heat. Pour over the chutney and serve.

Saunth

Ingredients

Dry ginger *(sonth)* powder 6 gms / 1 tsp
Sugar 250 gms / 1⅓ cup
Dry mango *(amchoor)* powder 100 gms / ½ cup
White pepper powder 5 gms / 1 tsp
Red chilli powder 10 gms / 2 tsp
Black rock salt *(kala namak)* 5 gms / 1 tsp
Garam masala (pg. 105) 3 gms / ½ tsp
Cumin *(jeera)* powder 3 gms / ½ tsp
Fennel *(saunf)* powder 3 gms / ½ tsp
Water 175 ml / ¾ cups

Method

1 Mix together all the ingredients to a smooth paste.

2 Strain through a strainer and transfer to a serving dish. Serve cold.

Mint Chutney

Serves: 4

Preparation time: 20 minutes

Yellow Chutney

Serves: 4

Preparation time: 15 minutes

Saunth

Serves: 4

Preparation time: 15 minutes

Paneer (cottage cheese)

Red chilli paste

Tomato purée

COLD CUCUMBER SOUP

Serves: 4

Preparation time: 30 minutes

Cooking time: 45 minutes

Exotic Lamb Soup

Ingredients

Lamb, bones 1 kg
Wheat 100 gms / ½ cup
Water 2 litres / 10 cups
Garam masala, whole 10 gms / 2 tsp
Bayleaf *(tej patta)* 1
Onions, pounded 10 gms / 2 tsp
Garlic, chopped 10 gms / 2 tsp
Ginger, chopped 10 gms / 2 tsp
White butter 45 gms / 3 tbs
Onions, chopped 45 gms / 3 tbs
Almond paste 45 gms / 3 tbs
Salt to taste
White pepper powder 3 gms / ½ tsp
Saffron *(kesar)* a few strands

For garnishing:

Lamb brunoise, boiled 45 gms / 3 tbs

Method

1 Soak wheat in sufficient water overnight and squeeze out the wheat milk.

2 Heat water (2 litres / 10 cups) in a *handi* (pot), add the lamb bones, garam masala, bayleaf, onion, garlic, ginger and allow to cook for about 4-5 hours on low heat. Remove from heat and strain through a soup strainer.

3 Melt butter in a pan and sauté the onions till slightly browned. Stir in the strained stock, cook for 5-10 minutes.

4 Add the almond paste and allow to cook for 5 minutes. Stir in the salt and white pepper powder. Remove from heat and strain the stock.

5 Reheat the stock in a *handi* (pot), add saffron and wheat milk. Bring to a boil and remove from heat.

6 Serve hot, garnished with boiled lamb brunoise.

EXOTIC LAMB SOUP

Serves: 4

Preparation time: 12-14 hours

Cooking time: 5 hours

Spinach Soup

Ingredients

Spinach *(palak)* 500 gms / 2 ½ cups
Butter 30 gms / 2 tbs
Flour 30 gms / 2 tbs
Ginger, chopped 25 gms / 5 tsp
Garlic, chopped 5 gms / 1 tsp
Black peppercorns 3 gms / ½ tsp
Bayleaves *(tej patta)* 4
Salt to taste
White pepper powder a pinch
Vegetable stock 1 ½ litres / 7 cups

Method

1 Chop the spinach leaves into small pieces and wash thoroughly.

2 Melt buttter in a *handi* (pot). Add flour and cook to a sandy texture.

3 Add ginger, garlic, spinach and sauté for a few minutes. Add black peppercorns and bayleaves.

4 Stir in the salt, white pepper powder and vegetable stock. Simmer for 15-20 minutes.

5 Remove the spinach from the stock and blend to a purée. Return the spinach purée to the stock and cook for 5 minutes.

6 Remove from heat, transfer to soup bowls and serve hot.

SPINACH SOUP

Serves: 4

Preparation time: 20 minutes

Cooking time: 30 minutes

Carrot and Orange Soup

Ingredients

Carrots, cut into small cubes
500 gms / 2 ½ cups
Orange juice 800 ml / 4 cups
Butter 25 gms / 5 tsp
Onions, chopped 150 gms / ¾ cup
Salt to taste
White pepper powder 3 gms / ½ tsp
Sugar 45 gms / 3 tbs
Cream 100 gms / ½ cup

Method

1 Heat butter in a pan, add the onion and sauté till transparent.

2 Add the carrots and sauté for a minute. Add the remaining ingredients except cream and cook on low heat till the carrot pieces are tender.

3 Remove and pass through a soup strainer and then strain through a muslin cloth.

4 Reheat the strained soup and stir in the cream.

5 Remove from heat and transfer to soup bowls. Serve hot.

CARROT AND ORANGE SOUP

Serves: 4

Preparation time: 1 hour

Cooking time: 40 minutes

Tomato and Coconut Soup

Ingredients

Tomatoes,chopped 500 gms / 2 ½ cups
Coconut, grated 100 gms / ½ cup
Coconut oil 45 ml / 3 tbs
Garlic, chopped 10 gms / 2 tsp
Onions, chopped 45 gms / 3 tbs
Ginger, crushed 15 gms / 1 tbs
Salt to taste
White pepper powder 3 gms / ½ tsp
Bayleaves *(tej patta)* 4
Vegetable stock 1 ½ litres / 7 cups
Cream 45 gms / 3 tbs

Method

1 Heat coconut oil in a *handi* (pot). Sauté garlic and onions for a few seconds.

2 Add coconut and stir-fry. Add tomatoes and ginger.

3 Stir in the salt, white pepper powder, bayleaves and vegetable stock. Allow to simmer for 15-20 minutes till the tomatoes are cooked and tender.

4 Remove from heat and allow to cool.

5 Blend to obtain a purée, strain through a muslin cloth and reheat.

6 Remove from heat and stir in the cream.

7 Transfer to soup bowl and serve immediately.

Tomato and Coconut Soup

Serves: 4

Preparation time: 15 minutes

Cooking time: 30 minutes

Tangy Yoghurt Soup

Ingredients

Yoghurt 300 gms / 1½ cups
Butter 25 gms / 5 tbs
Fenugreek *(methi)* seeds 10 gms / 2 tsp
Mustard *(raee)* seeds 10 gms / 2 tsp
Gramflour *(besan)* 150 gms / ¾ cup
Salt to taste
White pepper powder 5 gms / 1 tsp
Turmeric *(haldi)* powder 5 gms / 1 tsp
White radish, peeled, cut into cubes 225 gms / 1 cup
Water 3 litres / 15 cups
Curry leaves 10 gms / 2 tsp
Curry powder 5 gms / 1 tsp
Cream 100 gms/ ½ cup

Method

1 Melt butter in a *handi* (pot), add fenugreek and mustard seeds, sauté till they crackle, add gramflour, salt, white pepper powder, turmeric powder, and radish blended in yoghurt.

2 Add water (1 litre / 5 cups) and cook till a pleasing smell of gramflour emanates. Reduce heat and simmer for 10 minutes.

3 Add the remaining water and curry leaves, cook on low heat till it comes to a boil. Stir in the curry powder.

4 Remove from heat and pass through a soup strainer.

5 Stir in the cream, transfer to soup bowls and serve.

TANGY YOGHURT SOUP

Serves: 4

Preparation time: 15 minutes

Cooking time: 25 minutes

Tomato and Coriander Soup

Ingredients

Tomatoes, chopped 500 gms / 2½ cups
Butter 30 gms / 2 tbs
Coriander seeds 3 gms / ½ tsp
Ginger, chopped 5 gms / 1 tsp
Garlic, chopped 5 gms / 1 tsp
Flour 45 gms / 3 tbs
Bayleaves *(tej patta)* 4
Salt 15 gms / 1 tbs
White pepper powder 3 gms / ½ tsp
Vegetable stock 1½ litre / 7 cups
Orange/Red colour 5 gms / 1 tsp
Green coriander, chopped
20 gms / 4 tsp

Method

1 Melt butter in a *handi* (pot), add coriander seeds and sauté till they crackle. Add ginger and garlic and sauté for a minute.

2 Add flour and cook to a sandy texture without colouring, add the tomatoes and sauté for a few minutes.

3 Stir in the remaining ingredients except green coriander and cook for about 20 minutes.

4 Remove from heat and pass through a soup strainer.

5 Add the green coriander and reheat till it comes to a boil.

6 Remove from heat and transfer to soup bowls.

7 Serve immediately, garnished with green coriander.

TOMATO AND CORIANDER SOUP

Serves: 4

Preparation time: 15 minutes

Cooking time: 35 minutes

BARBECUED CHICKEN DRUMSTICKS

Ingredients

Chicken drumsticks (skinless) 15
Lemon juice 25 ml / 5 tsp
Cumin powder, roasted 5 gms / 1 tsp
Garam masala (pg. 105) 10 gms / 2 tsp
Garlic paste (pg. 105) 20 gms / 4 tsp
Ginger paste (pg. 105) 20 gms / 4 tsp
Red chilli powder 7 gms / 1½ tsp
Salt to taste
Yoghurt 200 gms / 1 cup
Butter / Oil for basting

Method

1 Make 2 incisions on each drumstick.

2 Rub lemon juice into the drumsticks. Keep aside for 20 minutes.

3 Mix all ingredients except butter/oil into the yoghurt and mix well.

4 Add chicken to the marinade and coat the pieces evenly. Keep aside for 2-3 hours.

5 Preheat oven/grill to 175 °C (350 °F).

6 Skewer drumsticks 2 cm apart and roast/grill in tandoor/ oven for 10-12 minutes. Baste with melted butter/oil 2-3 times. Roast until golden brown in colour.

7 Serve hot, on a bed of shredded lettuce/cabbage garnished with onion rings, tomato slices and lemon wedges.

BARBECUED CHICKEN DRUMSTICKS

Serves: 4-5

Preparation time: 3-4 hours

Cooking time: 15-20 minutes

Chicken Tikka

Ingredients

Chicken breasts, cut into boneless cubes 4
Yoghurt 150 ml / ¾ cup
Garlic paste (pg. 105) 5 gms / 1 tsp
Ginger, finely chopped 8 gms / 1½ tsp
Onion (small), grated 1
Red chilli powder 8 gms / 1½ tsp
Coriander powder 15 gms / 1 tbs
Salt to taste
Butter for basting

Method

1 Combine yoghurt, garlic paste, ginger, onion, chilli powder, coriander and salt together in a bowl and mix well. Add chicken cubes to the marinade and coat evenly. Cover the bowl and refrigerate for at least 6 hours or overnight.

2 Skewer the chicken cubes, roast in a preheated grill/ tandoor, turning them occasionally for 8-10 minutes or until cooked through, basting at least once.

3 Remove kababs from skewers and place on a warmed serving dish. Garnish with onion rings, tomato slices and coriander leaves. Serve at once, accompanied by Mint Chutney, (page 102).

CHICKEN TIKKA

Serves: 3-4

Preparation time: 6 hours 30 minutes

Cooking time: 10 minutes

Ginger Chicken Kababs

Ingredients

Chicken breasts, cut into boneless cubes 1kg
Green chilli paste 15 gms / 1 tbs
White pepper 10 gms / 2 tsp
Salt to taste
Ginger paste (pg. 105) 60 gms / 4 tbs
Malt vinegar 20 ml / 4 tsp
Yoghurt, drained 200 gms / 1 cup
Cream 60 gms / 4 tbs
Butter for basting
Ginger, julienned 10 gms / 2 tsp

Method

1 Clean the chicken cubes. Mix green chilli paste, white pepper powder, salt, ginger paste and vinegar in a large bowl, rub into the chicken cubes. Keep aside for 30 minutes.

2 Mix yoghurt with cream in a seperate bowl. Add the chicken cubes to the mixture and keep aside for ½ hour.

3 Skewer chicken cubes and roast in a preheated 175 °C (350 °F) oven/tandoor/grill for 5-8 minutes. Hang skewers to allow excess liquids to drip. Roast again for 4-5 minutes. Remove from skewers.

4 Serve hot, garnished with julienned ginger and accompanied by Mint Chutney, (page 102).

Ginger Chicken Kababs

Serves:4

Preparation time: 1 hour 30 minutes

Cooking time: 15 minutes

Chicken Seekh Kabab

Ingredients

Chicken, minced 1 kg
Eggs 2
Cumin *(jeera)* powder 15 gms / 1 tbs
Yellow chilli powder 5 gms / 1 tsp
White pepper powder 5 gms / 1 tsp
Salt to taste
Oil 20 ml / 4 tsp
Cashewnuts, pounded 60 gms / 4 tbs
Ginger, finely chopped 30 gms / 2 tbs
Onions, finely chopped 20 gms / 4 tsp
Coriander, finely chopped 20 gms / 4 tsp
Garam masala (pg. 105) 5 gms / 1 tsp
Oil for basting
Butter (unsalted) for brushing

Method

1 Whisk the eggs, add cumin powder, yellow chilli powder, white pepper powder, salt and oil (4 tsp). Add to the mince and mix well. Keep aside for 10 minutes.

2 Add cashewnuts, ginger, onions, coriander and garam masala. Mix well.

3 Divide into 10 equal portions.

4 Wrap two portions along each skewer using wet hands. Keep 2 inches between each portion. Prepare 5 skewers like this.

5 Roast in a moderately hot tandoor or charcoal grill until golden brown in colour, about 6 minutes or roast in a preheated oven at 150 °C (300 °F) for 8 minutes, basting with oil just once.

6 Remove from skewers and brush with butter.

7 Serve hot, garnished with onion rings and lemon wedges.

CHICKEN SEEKH KABAB

Serves: 4

Preparation time: 30 minutes

Cooking time: 6 minutes

Colourful Chicken Seekh Kabab

Ingredients

Chicken, minced 800 gms
Eggs, whisked 2
Cumin powder *(jeera)* 10 gms / 2 tsp
Yellow chilli powder (deghi mirch) 5 gms / 1 tsp
White pepper powder 5 gms / 1 tsp
Salt to taste
Oil 45 ml / 3 tbs
Cashewnut paste 45 gms / 3 tbs
Ginger, chopped 20 gms / 4 tsp
Green chillies, chopped 15 gms / 1 tbs
Garlic paste (pg. 105) 20 gms / 4 tsp
Green coriander, chopped 15 gms / 3 tsp
Onions, chopped fine 10 gms / 2 tsp
Cottage cheese *(paneer)* (pg. 105), grated 60 gms / 4 tbs
Garam masala (pg. 105) 5 gms / 1 tsp
Capsicum *(green pepper)*, chopped fine 10 gms / 2 tsp
Tomatoes, chopped fine 10 gms / 2 tsp
Butter for basting 60 gms / 4 tbs
Chaat masala 5 gms / 1 tsp
Lemon juice 30 ml / 2 tbs

Method

1 Add the whisked eggs, cumin powder, yellow chillies powder, white pepper powder, salt and oil to the minced chicken, and mix well. Keep aside for 15 minutes.

2 Add to the chicken mince the cashewnut paste, ginger, green chillies, garlic paste, green coriander, onions, paneer and garam masala, and mix well.

3 Divide into 8 equal portions and make into balls. Skewer the balls of mince. With wet hands spread the balls by pressing each along the length of the skewers to make 10 cm long kababs, 4 cm apart.

4 Mix capsicum, tomato and gently press over the skewers evenly from top to bottom.

5 Roast in a hot oven to 175 °C (350 °F) for 8-10 minutes, basting melted butter and roast until golden brown.

6 Sprinkle chaat masala and lemon juice, and serve, garnished with onion rings and lemon wedges.

Colourful Chicken Seekh Kabab

Serves: 4-5

Preparation time: 20 minutes

Cooking time: 8-10 minutes

Chicken Spring Rolls

Ingredients

For the stuffing:

Chicken, boneless (cut into 1.25 cm x 1.25 cm or ½" x ½") 500 gms
Cottage cheese (paneer), grated 50 gms / ¼ cup
Garam masala (pg. 105) 10 gms / 2 tsp
Ginger, chopped 30 gms / 2 tbs
Green chillies, chopped 10 gms / 2 tsp
Green coriander, chopped 10 gms / 2 tsp
Lemon juice 20 ml / 1 1/3 tbs
Oil 30 ml / 2 tbs, Salt to taste
Onions, chopped 50 gms / ¼ cup
White pepper powder 5 gms / 1 tsp

For the romali rotis (6):

Eggs, beaten 2, Flour 250 gms / 1 ¼ cups
Milk 200 ml / 1 cup, Oil 50 gms / 3 1/3 tbs
Oil for deep frying 500 ml / 2 ½ cups
Salt to taste, Sugar 3 gms / 2/3 tsp

Method

1 **For the filling,** heat the oil in a pan, add the ginger and onions and sauté over medium heat for 30 seconds.

2 Add the chicken, white pepper powder, garam masala, green chillies and green coriander and cook on low heat stirring occasionally. When the chicken is cooked add the paneer, salt and lemon juice.

3 **For the romali rotis,** seive flour. Make a depression in the centre and pour the milk, sugar, salt, oil and the beaten eggs.

4 Mix gradually to make a soft dough. Cover with a moist cloth and keep aside for half an hour. Knead the dough again. Make 6 balls, dust with flour, cover and keep aside for 15 minutes.

5 Flatten each ball between the palms and roll into thin 24 cm or 12"-round discs.

6 Preheat the oven to 175 °C (350 °F) and bake the rotis on a roasting tray for 3-4 minutes. Bake on both sides.

7 Cut each roti into 6 pieces. Stuff each roti piece with the stuffing, shape like a cigar and seal edges with water. Deep fry 10 pieces at a time.

8 Serve, accompanied by a green salad.

Chicken Spring Rolls

Serves: 4-5

Preparation time: 1 hour

Cooking time: 30 minutes

Egg and Cheese Coated Chicken Legs

Ingredients

Chicken drumsticks, skinned and deboned 5
Nutmeg powder *(jaiphal)* 3 gms / ½ tsp
Black pepper, crushed 5 gms / 1 tsp
Garam masala (pg. 105) 5 gms / 1 tsp
Green chilli paste 5 gms / 1 tsp
Cornflour 20 gms / 4 tsp
Cottage cheese *(paneer)* (pg. 105), grated 60 gms / 4 tbs
Cream 45 ml / 3 tbs
Eggs 2
Lemon juice 3 ml / ½ tsp
Mace powder *(javitri)* 3 gms / ½ tsp
Salt to taste
Yoghurt, hung 75 gms / 5 tbs
Butter 45 gms / 3 tbs
Clarified butter *(ghee)* 100 gms / ½ cup

Method

1 With a steak hammer flatten the deboned chicken drumsticks and arrange them on a platter.

2 Make a paste of the nutmeg powder, black pepper, garam masala and green chillies paste. Rub the paste on the chicken pieces. Keep aside for an hour.

3 In a bowl combine all the other ingredients to a fine creamy consistency.

4 Marinate the chicken in this mixture for further half an hour

5 Heat the clarified butter *(ghee)* in a pan over medium heat, and shallow fry the chicken pieces till crisp and golden.

6 Serve accompanied by lemon wedges, green salad and Mint Chutney, (page 102).

Egg and Cheese Coated Chicken Legs

Serves: 4-5

Preparation time: 1 hour 30 minutes

Cooking time: 15 minutes

Chicken Kabab with Nuts

Ingredients

Chicken legs, whole 4
Chicken, minced 300 gms
Almonds 45 gms / 3 tbs
Cashewnuts 45 gms / 3 tbs
Cream 100 ml / ½ cup
Garam masala (pg. 105) 5 gms / 1 tsp
Garlic paste (pg. 105) 25 gms / 5 tsp
Ginger paste (pg. 105) 25 gms / 5 tsp
Green chilli paste 25 gms / 5 tsp
Groundnut oil 15 ml / 1 tbs
Lemon juice 30 ml / 2 tbs
Lemon wedges and tomato slices for garnishing
Mint chutney (pg. 102) 100 gms / ½ cup
Saffron a few strands
Salt to taste

Method

1 Debone the entire chicken leg, leaving only the top of the drumstick. Flatten the chicken leg using a steak hammer.

2 Make a marinade with half the quantity of ginger and garlic paste, salt, green chilli paste and lemon juice. Marinate the chicken in this and refrigerate for half an hour.

3 Chop the almonds and cashewnuts and mix with the chicken mince and chutney.

4 Add garam masala and the remaining ginger, garlic, green chilli pastes, salt and lemon juice to the mince mixture and mix well.

5 Stuff the deboned chicken with this mixture, rolling the chicken in such a way that the mince is wrapped in it.

6 Grease a baking tray with the groundnut oil. Place the rolls on the tray and cover with foil. Bake in a medium oven to 100 °C (200 °F) until done (approximately 20 minutes).

7 Take the chicken out of the oven and remove the foil. Slice each chicken roll diagonally and arrange on a platter.

8 Pour the saffron mixed with cream over the sliced chicken.

9 Serve hot, garnished with lemon wedges and tomato slices.

CHICKEN KABAB WITH NUTS

Serves: 4-5

Preparation time: 45 minutes

Cooking time: 20 minutes

Chicken Kababs

Ingredients

Chicken, cut into boneless cubes 900 gms
Salt 10 gms / 2 tsp
Dry fenugreek *(kasoori methi)* powder 3 gms / ½ tsp
Ginger-garlic paste (pg. 105) 30 gms /2 tbs
Green chillies, chopped 10 gms / 2 tsp
Green coriander, chopped 10 gms /2 tsp
Vinegar 5 gms / 1 tsp
Oil 75 ml / 5 tbs
Gramflour *(besan)*, seived 25 gms / 5 tsp
Bread crumbs, fresh 45 gms / 3 tbs
Egg (yolks only), whisked 6

Method

1 Wash and dry the chicken cubes. Add salt, dry fenugreek powder, ginger-garlic paste, green chillies, green coriander alongwith vinegar to the cubes and mix thoroughly. Refrigerate for 15 minutes.

2 Heat oil in a pan, add gramflour and stir-fry till a pleasing smell emanates. Add the chicken cubes and sauté on low heat for 3-5 minutes till they are half cooked.

3 Add breadcrumbs and mix well. Remove and spread on a clean table top. Allow to cool.

4 Skewer the cubes 2" apart and roast in a tandoor till done. Bring the cubes close together and coat with egg yolks.

5 Roast in the tandoor till the egg yolk coating turns golden brown in colour. Remove from the skewer and serve hot, garnished with onion rings and accompained by Mint Chutney, (page 102).

CHICKEN KABABS

Serves: 4

Preparation time: 45 minutes

Cooking time: 20 minutes

Stuffed Chicken Steaks

Ingredients

Chicken necks, outer skin only, without the centre neck bone, cleaned thoroughly 5 pieces or Chicken breasts, skinned and flattened with a steak hammer 5 pieces

Chicken, minced 900 gms

Aniseed powder 3 gms / ½ tsp

Cheese, grated 25 gms / 5 tsp

Black pepper powder 5 gms / 1 tsp

Butter to baste 100 gms / ½ cup

Cream 20 ml / 4 tsp

Egg 1

Garam masala (pg. 105) 10 gms / 2 tsp

Garlic paste (pg. 105) 30 gms / 2 tbs

Ginger paste (pg. 105) 30 gms / 2 tbs

Green chilli paste 8 gms / 1 ½ tsp

Green coriander, chopped 10 gms / 2 tsp

Lemon juice 15 ml / 1 tbs

Nutmeg *(jaiphal)*, grated ½

Onions, grated 45 gms / 3 tbs

Salt to taste

Method

1 Mix all the ingredients except for the chicken necks or chicken breasts, with the chicken mince, and keep in the refrigerator for 30 minutes.

2 Divide the mixture into 5 portions, and make into balls for stuffing the breast or neck.

3 Stuff each neck right through with a portion of the mixture and tie a thread on both ends of the stuffed necks. Or if using breasts, place each ball in the centre of the chicken breast, wrap, shape like a haggis, and tie with the kitchen thread.

4 Heat the oven to 150 °C (300 °F).

5 Grease the roasting tray, arrange the stuffed necks or stuffed chicken breasts on it and dot with a little butter. Roast for 30-40 minutes, turning constantly and basting with melted butter, until the skins are golden in colour.

6 Remove the threads, arrange the chicken on a serving platter and serve hot with green salads and Mint Chutney, (page 102).

STUFFED CHICKEN STEAKS

Serves: 4-5

Preparation time: 40 minutes

Cooking time: 40 minutes

Tandoori Chicken Chaat

Ingredients

Tandoori chicken, shredded 2
Lemon juice 15 ml / 1 tbs
Salt to taste
Red chilli powder 3 gms / ½ tsp
Oil 15 ml / 1 tbs
Raw green mango 100 gms / ½ cup
Onions, finely sliced 100 gms / ½ cup
Green chillies, chopped 10 gms / 2 tsp
Green coriander, chopped 45 gms / 3 tbs
Chaat masala 10 gms / 2 tsp
Ginger, chopped 5 gms / 1 tsp

Method

1 Prepare a lemon dressing by mixing together the lemon juice alongwith salt, red chilli powder and oil. Keep aside.

2 Cut the raw mango into strips.

3 In a mixing bowl, add mango, onions, green chillies, green coriander, chaat masala alongwith the shredded chicken and the lemon dressing. Mix well.

4 Remove to a serving bowl and serve immediately, garnished with chopped ginger.

TANDOORI CHICKEN CHAAT

Serves: 4

Preparation time: 10 minutes

Cooking time: 10 minutes

Lamb Seekh Kabab

Ingredients

Lamb, minced 900 gms / 4½ cups
Green coriander, finely chopped 10 gms / 2 tsp
Green cardamom powder 3 gms / ½ tsp
Cottage cheese *(paneer)* (pg. 105), grated 15 gms / 1 tbs
Garam masala (pg. 105) 20 gms / 4 tsp
Ginger paste (pg. 105) 45 gms / 3 tbs
Green chillies, finely chopped 8 gms / 1½ tsp
Lamb kidney fat 150 gms / ¾ cup
Mace powder *(javitri)* 5 gms / 1 tsp
Onion paste, browned (pg. 105) 100 gms / ½ cup
Poppy seed *(khus khus)* paste 100 gms / ½ cup
Salt to taste
Butter to baste 60 gms / 4 tbs

Method

1 Combine all the ingredients in a bowl, mix thoroughly and refrigerate for 15 minutes.

2 Divide into 20 equal portions and roll into balls.

3 Preheat oven to 175 °C (350 °F).

4 Skewer each ball. Spread by pressing each, along the length of the skewer with a wet hand, making each kabab 8-10 cms long, 4 cms apart.

5 Roast in a hot tandoor or oven or charcoal grill for 8-10 minutes.

6 Remove and hang the skewers to let the excess moisture drip off.

7 Baste with butter and roast for another 2 minutes.

8 Garnish with sliced cucumber, tomato slices and onion rings. Serve hot, accompanied by Mint Chutney (page 102).

Lamb Seekh Kabab

Serves: 4-5

Preparation time: 25 minutes

Cooking time: 15 minutes

Exotic Lamb Kababs

Ingredients

Lamb, minced 250 gms / 1 ¼ cup
Lamb kidney, finely chopped 125 gms / ¾ cup
Lamb liver, finely chopped 125 gms / ¾ cup
Salt 3 gms / ½ tsp
Red chilli powder 3 gms / ½ tsp
Garam masala (pg. 105) 3 gms / ½ tsp
Fenugreek *(methi)* powder a pinch
Ginger-garlic paste (pg. 105) 10 gms / 2 tsp
Green coriander, chopped 5 gms / 1 tsp
Green chillies, chopped 5 gms / 1 tsp
Chicken, minced 500 gms / 2½ cups
Salt 3 gms / ½ tsp
White pepper powder 3 gms / ½ tsp
Garam masala (pg. 105) a pinch
Fenugreek *(methi)* powder a pinch
Ginger-garlic paste (pg. 105) 3 gms / ½ tsp
Green coriander, chopped 5 gms / 1 tsp
Butter for basting 20 gms / 4 tsp

Method

1 Mix together the lamb mince, kidney, liver, salt, red chilli powder, garam masala, fenugreek powder, ginger-garlic paste, green coriander and green chillies. Keep aside.

2 Skewer the lamb mince mixture and roast in a charcoal grill for 8-10 minutes. Remove from the charcoal grill, place skewer upright to allow excess liquids to drip. Keep aside for 3-5 minutes.

3 Meanwhile, mix chicken mince alongwith all the other ingredients.

4 Apply a coating of the chicken mince mixture evenly onto the lamb mince kababs and roast again for 5-6 minutes.

5 Baste with butter and remove the kababs from skewers in 4 equal portions.

6 Serve immediately, accompained by a green salad and Mint Chutney, (page 102).

Exotic Lamb Kababs

Serves: 4

Preparation time: 1 hour

Cooking time: 20-25 minutes

Cocktail Kababs

Ingredients

Lamb, minced ½ kg
Split grams (chana daal)
115 gms / ½ cup
Red chillies, dried and chopped 4-5
Onions (medium), chopped 2
Salt to taste
Ginger, chopped 10 gms / 2 tsp
Garam masala (pg. 105) 8 gms / 1½ tsp
Egg, slightly beaten 1

For the Filling:

Coriander leaves, chopped 6 gms / 1 tsp
Green chillies, finely chopped
15 gms / 1 tbs
Onions, finely chopped 60 gms / 4 tbs
Salt to taste
Oil for frying

Method

1 Boil minced meat alongwith split grams, red chillies, onions, salt and ginger in 4 cups of water till meat and gram is tender. Strain the liquid completely.

2 Grind the mince very finely, add the garam masala powder and beaten egg and knead well. Divide into 20 equal portions and keep aside.

3 **For the the filling,** mix chopped onions, green chillies, coriander leaves, salt and divide into 20 equal parts.

4 Flatten each part of the mince, put one part of stuffing into the centre and shape into a ball, wetting hands with water.

5 Heat oil in flat pan till it is smoking hot. Deep fry kababs, a few at a time till crispy and brown.

6 Serve hot, garnished with onion rings and accompanied by Mint Chutney, (page 102).

Cocktail Kababs

Serves: 4-6

Preparation time: 1 hour 30 minutes

Cooking time: 30 minutes

Fenugreek Flavoured, Grilled Lamb Cubes

Ingredients

Lamb (leg or shoulder), cut into boneless cubes 1 kg
Ginger paste (pg. 105) 45 gms / 3 tbs
Garlic paste (pg. 105) 45 gms / 3 tbs
Vinegar 45 ml / 3 tbs
Red chilli powder 10 gms / 2 tsp
Black pepper, ground 5 gms / 1 tsp
Salt to taste
Cream 45 gms / 3 tbs
Cheese 45 gms / 3 tbs
Garam masala (pg. 105) 5 gms / 1 tsp
Cumin *(jeera)* powder 5 gms / 1 tsp
Saffron *(kesar)* a pinch
Dry fenugreek *(kasoori methi)* powder 3 gms / ½ tsp
Butter for basting

Method

1 Mix ginger, garlic, vinegar, red chilli powder, black pepper and salt together.

2 Marinate the lamb cubes in the prepared mixture for 2 hours.

3 In another bowl, mix cream, cheese, garam masala, cumin powder, saffron and fenugreek powder together. Add marinated lamb to this mixture, set aside for 1 hour.

4 Preheat oven to 175 °C (350 °F). Skewer the lamb cubes, 2 cms apart. Roast in the oven/charcoal grill/tandoor for 8-10 minutes. Hang the skewers for a few minutes to allow excess liquids to drip. Baste with butter and cook further for another 3-4 minutes.

5 Serve hot, garnished with chopped coriander and cream, accompanied by lemon wedges and onion rings.

Fenugreek Flavoured, Grilled Lamb Cubes

Serves: 4-5

Preparation time: 3 hours 30 minutes

Cooking time: 20 minutes

Barbecued Lamb Cubes

Ingredients

Lamb (leg piece, chopped in boneless pieces) 1 kg
Yoghurt 150 ml / ¾ cup
Coriander powder 10 gms / 2 tsp
Turmeric powder 10 gms / 2 tsp
Red chilli powder 3 gms / ½ tsp
Ginger paste (pg. 105) 25 gms / 5 tsp
Garlic paste (pg. 105) 25 gms / 5 tsp
Salt to taste
Oil for basting

Method

1 Mix together yoghurt, coriander powder, turmeric powder, red chilli powder, ginger and garlic pastes and salt.

2 Pour mixture over lamb and coat the pieces evenly.

3 Baste the marinated pieces with oil and cover the bowl. Chill in refrigerator for 5-6 hrs, basting occasionally.

4 Preheat grill/oven to 175 °C (350 °C).

5 Mix meat marinade well, then skewer the pieces 2 cm apart.

6 Roast in tandoor/grill for 5-8 minutes on each side or until cooked through, basting just once.

7 Serve hot, on a warmed serving dish garnished with onion rings, chopped coriander and lemon wedges, accompanied by Mint Chutney (page 102).

BARBECUED LAMB CUBES

Serves: 4-5

Preparation time: 6-7 hours

Cooking time: 10 minutes

Yoghurt Flavoured Lamb Kabab

Ingredients

Lamb (cut into boneless cubes) 1 kg
Salt to taste
Red chilli powder 10 gms / 2 tsp
Garam masala (pg. 105) 5 gms / 1 tsp
Raw papaya paste 10 gms / 2 tsp
Black cumin *(shah jeera)* seeds 5 gms / 1 tsp
Ginger paste (pg. 105) 15 gms / 1 tbs
Garlic paste (pg. 105) 5 gms / 1 tsp
Yoghurt 120 gms / ½ cup
Clarified butter *(ghee)* for basting
Chaat masala 5 gms / 1 tsp
Lemon juice 7 gms / 1½ tsp

Method

1 Mix together, salt, red chilli powder, garam masala, papaya paste, black cumin, ginger and garlic pastes and yoghurt.

2 Marinade lamb cubes in mixture and put aside for 1 hour.

3 Skewer lamb cubes 2 cms apart and cook in a tandoor till half done. Leave to cool for 10 minutes.

4 Baste with clarified butter *(ghee)* and roast for 8 more minutes or until done.

5 Sprinkle chaat masala and lemon juice. Serve hot, accompanied by a green salad.

YOGHURT FLAVOURED LAMB KABAB

Serves: 4

Preparation time: 1 hour 15 minutes

Cooking time: 30 minutes

Barbecued Liver

Ingredients

Liver, cut into cubes 250 gms
Ginger paste (pg. 105) 15 gms /1tbs
Garlic paste (pg. 105) 5 gms / 1 tsp
Onion paste (pg. 105) 5 gms / 1 tsp
Yoghurt 30 gms / 2 tbs
Red chilli powder 3 gms / ½ tsp
Garam masala (pg. 105) 3 gms / ½ tsp
Cumin *(jeera)* powder 3 gms / ½ tsp
Green coriander, chopped 10 gms / 2 tsp
Turmeric *(haldi)* powder 3 gms / ½ tsp
Carom *(ajwain)* seeds 3 gms / ½ tsp
Dry fenugreek powder
(kasoori methi) 5 gms / 1 tsp
Salt to taste
Oil 15 ml / 1 tbs
Oil / Butter for basting

Method

1 Rub ginger, garlic and onion pastes into the liver cubes and set aside for an hour.

2 Mix the remaining ingredients into the yoghurt except oil/ butter for basting and evenly coat the liver cubes. Leave to marinate for at least 2 hours.

3 Preheat oven to 150 °C (300 °F).

4 Thread cubes gently onto the skewers. Roast/grill/bake till half done (10 minutes).

5 Drain excess liquids, baste once and roast again for 4-5 minutes till cooked through.

6 Serve at once, accompanied by salad and /or Mint Chutney, (page 102).

BARBECUED LIVER

Serves: 4-6

Preparation time: 3 hours 30 minutes

Cooking time: 30 minutes

Sesame Prawn Tikka

Ingredients

King Prawns 12
Lemon juice 10 gms / 2 tsp
Sesame *(til)* seeds 30 gms / 2 tbs
Oil 220 ml / 1¼ cup
Paprika 5 gms / 1 tsp
Garlic, crushed 5 gms / 1 tsp
Red chilli powder 3 gms / ½ tsp
Turmeric *(haldi)* powder 3 gms / ½ tsp
Salt to taste
Green coriander, chopped (optional)
5 gms / 1 tsp

Method

1 Wash, clean and devein prawns. Pat them dry. Rub lemon juice into the prawns. Set aside.

2 Coarsely grind (1tsp) sesame seeds. Put the rest aside to be used later for frying.

3 Mix the coarsely ground sesame seeds alongwith (1tsp) oil and the rest of the ingredients to form a marinadc. Coat the prawns in this marinade, cover the dish and put aside for 30 minutes.

4 Heat oil in a frying pan till it is smoking hot. Reduce fire to medium. Coat prawns evenly with remaining sesame seeds and deep fry till they are crisp and golden brown.

5 Garnish with chopped coriander and serve hot, accompanied by chilli sauce.

Sesame Prawn Tikka

Serves: 4-6

Preparation time: 45 minutes

Cooking time: 15 minutes

Prawn Cutlets

Ingredients

Prawns / Shrimps, shelled
and chopped 400 gms / 2 cups
Onions (medium), finely chopped 2
Ginger, chopped 15 gms / 1 tbs
Green chillies, chopped 2
Green coriander, chopped 15 gms / 1 tbs
Salt to taste
Lemon juice 5 gms / 1 tsp
Bread crumbs, dried, powdered
200 gms / 1 cup
Turmeric *(haldi)* powder 2 gms / ¼ tsp
Black pepper powder 3 gms / ½ tsp
Egg 1
Bread crumbs, fresh 200 gms / 1 cup
Oil for frying

Method

1 Mix together, the prawns/ shrimps, onions, ginger, chillies, coriander, salt, lemon juice, fresh bread crumbs, turmeric, black pepper and egg, knead well.

2 Divide mixture into eight portions and shape them into flat round cutlets.

3 Dip cutlets in dried bread crumbs, coating them evenly and brush off excess bread crumbs.

4 Heat oil in a *kadhai* (wok) till it is smoking. Lower cutlets gently into the oil and fry until they are golden brown, crisp and cooked through on each side.

5 Serve at once, accompanied by Mint Chutney, (page 102).

PRAWN CUTLETS

Serves: 4-6

Preparation time: 30 minutes

Cooking time: 30 minutes

Fish Tikka

Ingredients

Fish fillets, cut into cubes 1 kg
Salt to taste
Lemon juice 15 gms / 1 tbs
Yoghurt 120 gms / ½ cup
Vinegar 15 ml / 1 tbs
Garam masala (pg. 105) 15 gms / 1 tbs
Cumin *(jeera)* seeds, ground 10 gms / 2 tsp
Carom *(ajwain)* seeds 3 gms / ½ tsp
Red chilli powder 5 gms / 1 tsp
Garlic paste (pg. 105) 10 gms / 2 tsp
Oil / Butter for basting

Method

1 Wash and dry the cubed fish fillets. Sprinkle salt and lemon juice. Set aside to marinate for half an hour.

2 In a bowl, combine yoghurt with remaining ingredients and whisk well. Pour mixture over the fish cubes and coat evenly. Leave to marinate for at least one hour.

3. Preheat oven to 175 °C (350 °F).

4 Roast, bake or grill till the fillets are golden brown in colour and cooked through, basting just once.

5 Serve hot, accompanied by Mint Chutney, (page 102).

Fish Tikka

Serves: 4-6

Preparation time: 1 hour 30 minutes

Cooking time: 30 minutes

FISH KABABS

Ingredients

Fish fillets (3" x 2" x 1" pieces) 1 kg
Onions, finely chopped 175 gms / 3/5 cup
Malt vinegar 45 ml / 3 tbs
Green chillies,
finely chopped 25 gms / 5 tsp
Green coriander, finely chopped
15 gms / 1 tbs
Ginger, finely chopped 15 gms
Salt, Eggs 2
Bread crumbs, powdered
Oil / Clarified butter *(ghee)* for frying

Method

1 Wash fish fillets and dry completely on paper napkin or cloth.

2 Soak chopped onions in vineger for an hour, so that it gets absorbed into the onions. Add chopped green chillies, coriander, ginger and salt, mix well.

3 In a seperate bowl, beat egg lightly and keep aside.

4 Apply the onion mixture thinly and evenly on both sides of each fish fillet, dip into beaten eggs and then coat well with bread crumbs. Press lightly on both sides to make the coating firm. Refrigerate fish fillets for half an hour to allow the coating to dry.

5 Heat oil in a pan and fry each kabab on meduim heat till crisp and golden brown. Serve hot, accompanied by Mint Chutney, (page 102).

FISH KABABS

Serves: 6

Preparation time: 1 hour

Cooking time: 30 minutes

CHUTNEY FISH TIKKA

Ingredients

Fish fillets, cleaned and cut into cubes 1 kg
Yoghurt, drained 60 gms / 4 tbs
Cream 45 ml / 3 tbs
Garlic paste (pg. 105) 20 gms / 4 tsp
Carom *(ajwain)* seeds 8 gms / 1½ tsp
White pepper powder 3 gms / ½ tsp
Cumin *(jeera)* powder 10 gms / 2 tsp
Garam masala (pg. 105) 15 gms / 1 tbs
Salt to taste
Lemon juice 30 ml / 2 tbs
Mint or coriander chutney 135 ml / 3/4 cup
Gramflour / Rice flour 20 gms / 4 tsp
Butter / oil for basting

Method

1 Mix yoghurt with cream, garlic paste, carom seeds, white pepper, cumin powder, garam masala, salt, lemon juice, mint/ coriander chutney and gram/rice flour.

2 Add fish cubes to the marinade, coat evenly and set aside for 2-3 hrs.

3 Skewer fish 2 cms apart and roast in a pre-heated oven 175 °C (350 °F) or a tandoor for 8-10 minutes. Baste with butter once before roasting is complete.

4 Garnish with onion rings and serve hot.

CHUTNEY FISH TIKKA

Serves: 4-6

Preparation time: 3 hours 30 minutes

Cooking time: 15 minutes

Fish Rolls Stuffed with Prawns

Ingredients

Fish fillets, thin 12
Prawns, shelled, deveined 220 gms
Ginger-garlic paste (pg. 105) 25 gms / 5 tsp
Mango pickle masala 25 gms / 5 tsp
Carom *(ajwain)* seeds 3 gms / ½ tsp
White pepper powder 5 gms / 1 tsp
Garam masala (pg. 105) 5 gms / 1 tsp
Salt to taste
Red chilli powder 5 gms / 1 tsp
Lemon juice 5 gms / 1 tsp
Oil 20 ml / 4 tsp
Yoghurt, drained 180 gms / ¾ cup
Cream 30 gms / 2 tbs
Saffron *(kesar)* a few strands
Green cardamom *(choti elaichi)* powder a pinch
Water 1 ltr / 5 cups

Method

1 Extract juice from ginger-garlic paste and keep aside.

2 Clean the fish fillets and prawns. Pat dry with a cloth.

3 Make a marinade with half of carom seeds, white pepper powder, garam masala, salt, red chilli powder, lemon juice, extract of ginger-garlic paste, pickle masala and oil.

4 Marinate the fish fillets in the prepared marinade and keep aside for 5 minutes.

5 Prepare second marinade of yoghurt, cream, saffron, green cardamom powder and the remaining half of other ingredients.

6 Put one fish fillet flat on a table top. Place a prawn at one end of the fillet and roll the fillet.Wrap it tightly with cling wrap or aluminium foil.

7 Boil water in a handi (pot) and cook the rolls for 10 minutes keeping the pot covered.

8 Drain the water and place the rolls under running water for 1 minute. Remove the foil.

9 Marinate the rolls in the second marinade for 5 minutes.

10 Skewer the rolls and roast it in hot tandoor or in an oven (approx 300-350 °F) for 10 minutes. Remove from skewers, transfer to a serving platter and serve hot.

FISH ROLLS STUFFED WITH PRAWNS

Serves: 4

Preparation time: 40 minutes

Cooking time: 20 minutes

Tandoori Salad

Ingredients

Cottage cheese, cubed 160 gms / 3/4 cup
Chaat masala 20 gms / 4 tsp
Garam masala (pg. 105) 20 gms / 4 tsp
Lemon juice 15 ml / 1 tbs
Salt to taste
Salad oil 240 ml / 1 cup
Capsicum, deseeded and sliced
150 gms
Onions, sliced 160 gms / 3/4 cup
Tomatoes, halved
300 gms / 14-16 pieces
Pineapple slices, drained
480 gms / 2 cups
Lemon wedges 24

Method

1 Cut cottage cheese and pineapple slices into 1 inch cubes.

2 Add chaat masala, garam masala, lemon juice, salt and salad oil to the capsicum, onions and tomatoes. Toss well together.

3 Skewer the vegetables, cottage cheese and pineapple cubes in turn.

4 Cook on a slow grill for 10 minutes.

5 Remove from skewer onto a platter and serve with the lemon wedges.

TANDOORI SALAD

Serves: 4

Preparation time: 30 minutes

Cooking time: 15 minutes

STEAMED SAVORY GRAMFLOUR DISH

Ingredients

Gramflour *(besan)* 500 gms
Tartar powder 12 gms / 2 tsp
Water 400 ml / 2 cups
Oil 45 ml / 3 tbs
Vegetable soda 12 gms / 2 tsp
Cumin *(jeera)* seeds 10 gms / 2 tsp
Green chillies, chopped 10 gms / 2 tsp
Green coriander, chopped
45 gms / 3 tbs
Coconut, grated 120 gms / ½ cup
Lemons 2
Ginger, chopped 10 gms / 2 tsp
Salt 20 gms / 4 tsp
Mustard *(raee)* seeds 20 gms / 4 tsp
Green chillies, slit 30 gms / 2 tbs

Method

1 Dissolve tartar powder in water (50 ml).

2 Sieve gramflour in a bowl, add rest of the water to it and mix well to break all lumps. Add oil (1½ tbs), tartar dissloved in water and vegetable soda. Mix well.

3 Pour the gramflour mixture in a flat tray and steam for 15 minutes in a steamer or a double boiler with a lid on top. Remove and cool.

4 Make a fine paste by blending together the cumin seeds, green chillies, green coriander, coconut, juice of two lemons, ginger and salt. Keep aside.

5 Heat the remaining oil in a pan, add the mustard seeds and sauté till they crackle. Add slit green chillies, two cups of water. Bring to a boil and pour this over the cooked dhokla. Keep aside to soak.

6 Slice the dhokla into two portions. Apply the prepared paste evenly on one half and place the other half back on top.

7 Cut into square dices and serve.

STEAMED SAVORY GRAMFLOUR DISH

Serves: 4

Preparation time: 45 minutes

Cooking time: 30 minutes

GRAMFLOUR PANCAKES

Ingredients

Gramflour *(besan)* 150 gms / ¾ cup
Cumin *(zeera)* powder 5 gms / 1 tsp
Turmeric *(haldi)* powder 5 gms / 1 tsp
Red chilli powder 3 gms / ½ tsp
Salt to taste
Green chillies, chopped 5 gms / 1 tsp
Green coriander, chopped 10 gms / 2 tsp
Water as required
Cottage cheese *(paneer)* (pg. 105)
100 gms / ½ cup
Tomatoes, chopped 45 gms / 3 tbs
Onions, chopped 45 gms / 3 tbs
Oil for frying

Method

1 Mix gramflour, cumin seeds, turmeric powder, red chilli powder, salt, green chillies, green coriander and water to make a batter of spreading consistency.

2 Cut the cottage cheese into small cubes and mix with tomatoes and onions.

3 Heat a flat pan, brush with oil and spread batter to make a pancake of 7" diameter. Cook till crisp on both sides. Sprinkle little oil to avoid from sticking to pan.

4 Sprinkle some of the cottage cheese mixture on top and remove from heat.

5 Repeat the same process with the rest of the batter and cottage cheese mixture.

6 Serve hot, accompanied ny pickle.

GRAMFLOUR PANCAKES

Serves: 4

Preparation time: 30 minutes

Cooking time: 30 minutes

Stuffed Potato Cutlets

Ingredients

Potatoes, boiled, mashed 400 gms / 2 cups
Sultana (large raisins), chopped 45 gms / 3 tbs
Bread crumbs, fresh 25 gms / 5 tsp
White pepper powder 3 gms / ½ tsp
Salt 5 gms / 1 tsp
Green chillies, chopped 5 gms / 1 tsp
Green coriander, chopped 5 gms / 1 tsp
Ginger, chopped 3 gms / ½ tsp
Oil 75 ml / 5 tbs

Method

1 To the mashed potatoes, add bread crumbs, white pepper powder, salt, green chillies, green coriander and ginger.

2 Mix well and divide into 8 equal portions.

3 Divide the chopped raisins also into 8 equal portions.

4 Stuff the portion of the chopped raisins into one portion of the potato mixture and shape into medallion.

5 Heat a *tawa* (griddle), brush with oil and shallow fry the medallion until golden brown.

6 Drain excess oil and serve.

STUFFED POTATO CUTLETS

Serves: 4

Preparation time: 30 minutes

Cooking time: 30 minutes

Cauliflower Kabab

Ingredients

Cauliflower 400 gms / 2 cups
Potatoes 200 gms / 1 cup
Bread crumbs, fresh 60 gms / 4 tbs
Red chilli powder 5 gms / 1 tsp
Salt to taste
Chaat masala 5 gms / 1 tsp
Green chillies, finely chopped 5 gms / 1 tsp
Green coriander, finely chopped 5 gms / 1 tsp
Ginger, chopped 5 gms / 1 tsp
Oil 150 ml / ¾ cup

Method

1 Boil the cauliflower and potatoes separately. Drain excess water and allow to cool. Grate them separately.

2 Mix the grated cauliflower and grated potatoes alongwith bread crumbs, red chilli power, salt, chaat masala, green chillies, green coriander and ginger.

3 Divide into 16 equal portions and shape into medallion.

4 Heat a *tawa* (giddle), brush with oil and shallow fry the medallion a few at a time, until golden brown.

5 Drain excess oil and serve hot.

CAULIFLOWER KABAB

Serves: 4

Preparation time: 15 minutes

Cooking time: 15 minutes

Cottage Cheese Tikka

Ingredients

Cottage cheese *(paneer)* (pg. 105) 1 kg
Black cumin *(shah jeera)* 3 gms / ½ tsp
White pepper powder 5 gms / 1 tsp
Garam masala (pg. 105) 10 gms / 2 tsp
Turmeric *(haldi)* powder 5 gms / 1 tsp
Lemon juice 25 ml / 5 tsp
Salt to taste
Cream 150 ml / ¾ cup
Yoghurt, hung 150 gms / ¾ cup
Gramflour *(besan)* /cornflour
30 gms / 2 tbs
Cottage cheese *(paneer)* (pg. 105),
grated 60 gms / 4 tbs
Fenugreek *(methi)* 5 gms / 1 tsp
Garlic paste (pg. 105) 15 gms / 1 tbs
Ginger paste (pg. 105) 15 gms / 1 tbs
Red chilli powder 10 gms / 2 tsp
Saffron *(kesar)* 3 gms / ½ tsp
Butter to baste 50 gms / ¼ cup
Chaat masala 10 gms / 2 tsp

Method

1 Wash and cut the paneer into small cubes (30 pieces).

2 Mix the black cumin, white pepper powder, garam masala, turmeric powder, two-thirds of the lemon juice and salt. Sprinkle over the paneer cubes. Keep aside for 1 hour in the refrigerator.

3 Mix cream, yoghurt and gram flour / cornflour in a bowl. Add the remaining ingredients, whisk well to make a fine batter.

4 Add the paneer cubes to this and marinate for at least 1 hour.

5 Preheat the oven to 150-75 °C (300-50 °F).

6 Thread the paneer cubes on a skewer, 2 cm apart.

7 Roast in an oven, tandoor or on a charcoal grill for 5-6 minutes. Baste with melted butter.

8 Sprinkle with chaat masala and the remaining lemon juice.

Serve with a green salad and Mint Chutney (page 102).

COTTAGE CHEESE TIKKA

Serves: 4-5

Preparation time: 2 hours 15 minutes

Cooking time: 10 minutes

Cottage Cheese Croquettes

Ingredients

Cottage cheese *(paneer)* (pg. 105), grated 500 gms
Green chillies, chopped 4
Green coriander, chopped 15 gms / 1 tbs
White pepper 5 gms / 1 tsp
Red chilli powder 5 gms / 1 tsp
Carom *(ajwain)* seeds 3 gms / ½ tsp
Egg (optional) 1
Garam masala (pg. 105) 5 gms / 1 tsp
Oil for frying
Gramflour *(besan)* 75 gms / 5 tbs

Method

1 Combine grated cottage cheese and all other ingredients adding gramflour in the end and mix together in a bowl to make a smooth paste.

2 Shape the mixture into round croquettes/cutlets.

3 Heat oil in a *kadhai* (wok) till it is smoking. Slide in a few cutlets/croquettes at a time into the oil and fry till they are golden brown and crisp on all sides.

4 Serve hot, accompanied by Mint Chutney (page 102).

COTTAGE CHEESE CROQUETTES

Serves: 4

Preparation time: 10 minutes

Cooking time:15 minutes

Stuffed Cottage Cheese Tikka

Ingredients

Cottage cheese *(paneer)*, firm 500 gms
For the stuffing:
Black cumin *(shah jeera)* 5 gms / 1 tsp
Capsicum *(green pepper)*, chopped 150 gms / ¾ cup
Cayenne pepper *(kashmiri red chilli)* 10 gms / 2 tsp
Coconut powder 100 gms / ½ cup
Cottage cheese *(paneer)* (pg. 105), grated 150 gms / ¾ cup
Dry fenugreek *(kastoori methi)* 5 gms / 1 tsp
Lemon juice 10 ml / 2 tsp
Mushrooms, chopped 150 gms / ¾ cup
Oil 75 ml / 5 tbs
Onions, chopped 150 gms / ¾ cup
Potatoes, boiled and grated 100 gms / ½ cup
Raisins 100 gms / ½ cup
Salt to taste
Turmeric powder *(haldi)* 5 gms / 1 tsp
White pepper powder 20 gms / 4 tsp
For the coating:
Cornflour 100 gms / ½ cup
Cream 100 ml / ½ cup
Gramflour *(besan)* 45 gms / 3 tbs
Green coriander, chopped 20 gms / 4 tsp
Saffron a few strands
Water 20 ml / 4 tsp

Method

1 Slice the cottage cheese lengthwise into pieces of 15 cm x 6 cm x 0.5 cm.

2 Heat the oil. Add mushrooms, capsicum, onion and coconut powder and sauté.

3 Add the grated cottage cheese, potato and all the spices for the stuffing as well as the lemon juice.

4 Make a thick paste of gram flour and water for coating.

5 Smear the thick paste on one side of each cottage cheese slice, and on the other side put 70-80 gms of the stuffing and make into a roll.

6 Mix the remaining ingredients for the coating.

7 Coat the stuffed rolls with the coating and bake in a slow oven / tandoor for 10-12 minutes.

8 Sprinkle the tikkas with chaat masala and garnish with grated carrots and lemon wedges.

STUFFED COTTAGE CHEESE TIKKA

Serves: 4-5

Preparation time: 10 minutes

Cooking time: 20 minutes

Cottage Cheese Seekh Kabab

Ingredients

Cottage cheese, finely grated (pg. 105) 1 kg
Cornflour 15 gms / 1 tbs
Garam masala (pg. 105) 10 gms / 2 tsp
Ginger paste (pg. 105) 25 gms / 5 tsp
Green chillies, chopped 6
Lemon juice 15 ml / 1 tbs
Onions, grated 150 gms / ¾ cup
Red chilli powder 5 gms / 1 tsp
Salt for seasoning
White pepper powder 5 gms / 1 tsp
Butter for basting 20 gms / 4 tsp

Method

1 Mix all the ingredients, adding the cornflour in the end.

2 Divide this mixture into 15 equal balls.

3 Preheat the oven to 150-75 °C (300-50 °F).

4 Skewer each ball. Spread by pressing each along the length of the skewer with a wet hand, making each kabab about 8-10 cms long, 1 cm apart.

5 Roast in oven / tandoor / charcoal grill for 5-6 minutes, baste with melted butter and roast for another 2 minutes. Remove from skewers.

6. Garnish with slices of cucumber, tomato, onion and serve hot, accompanied by Mint Chutney (page 102).

COTTAGE CHEESE SEEKH KABAB

Serves: 4-5

Preparation time: 15 minutes

Cooking time: 15 minutes

POTATOES IN CHUTNEY

Ingredients

Potatoes, peeled 600 gms
Mint, fresh 5 gms / 1 tsp
Lemon juice 30 ml / 2 tbs
Green chillies 3
Green coriander, chopped
100 gms / ½ cup
Oil 100 ml / ½ cup
Ginger paste (pg. 105) 10 gms / 2 tsp
Garlic paste (pg. 105) 10 gms / 2 tsp
Cumin *(jeera)* powder 5 gms / 1 tsp
Coriander powder 8 gms / 1½ tsp
Red chilli paste 8 gms / 1½ tsp
Salt to taste

Method

1 Blend together fresh mint, lemon juice, green chillies and green coriander into a purée.

2 Heat oil in a heavy bottomed pan. Add ginger-garlic pastes and potatoes. Stir-fry for 2-3 minutes. Add cumin, coriander powder and red chilli paste. Stir-fry, add salt and water (250 ml). Bring to a boil and simmer till potatoes are cooked.

3 Add the blended purée and stir-fry for 4-5 minutes. Add salt and serve at once.

POTATOES IN CHUTNEY

Serves: 3-4

Preparation time: 20 minutes

Cooking time: 30 minutes

Potato Baskets

Ingredients

Potatoes (large), boiled and peeled 8
Chickpeas *(kabuli chana)*, boiled 150 gms / ¾ cup
Chaat masala 15 gms / 1 tbs
Ginger, finely chopped 15 gms / 1 tbs
Green chillies, finely chopped 10 gms / 2 tsp
Green coriander, finely chopped 15 gms / 1 tbs
Lemon juice 30 ml / 2 tbs
Salt to taste

Method

1. Cut potatoes in half and carefully scoop out the centres.
2. Mix together chickpeas, chaat masala, ginger, green chillies, coriander, lemon juice and salt, fill it in the centre of scooped potatoes. Serve on a flat dish.

Potato Baskets

Serves: 4-6

Preparation time:
5-6 minutes

Cooking time: 20 minutes

Tomatoes Stuffed with Mushrooms

Ingredients

Tomatoes (large) 6
Spring onions, chopped 60 gms / 4 tbs
Butter 15 gms / 1 tbs
Mushrooms, chopped 200 gms / 1 cup
Cream 15 gms / 1 tbs
Salt to taste
Green coriander, chopped 15 gms / 1 tbs
White pepper 5 gms / 1 tsp

Method

1 Slice each tomato at the top. Scoop out seeds and keep the tomato cup and top aside.

2 Sauté spring onions for two minutes in butter. Add mushrooms, cream, salt, coriander and pepper, sauté for 5 minutes. Remove and keep aside.

3 Drain excess moisture from mushrooms, carefully fill each tomato cup with the mushroom mixture. Cover with the top and secure with tooth-picks.

4 Preheat oven to 150 °C (300 °F). Place stuffed tomatoes on a baking tray and bake for 8-10 minutes. Remove tooth-picks and serve hot.

TOMATOES STUFFED WITH MUSHROOMS

Serve: 4-5

Preparation time: 30 minutes

Cooking time:10 minutes

Batter coated stuffed Tomatoes

Ingredients

Tomatoes 340-455 gms
Cottage cheese *(paneer)* (pg. 105)
140 gms / 3/5 cup
Black pepper, ground 1 gm / ¼ tsp
Asafoetida *(heeng)* powder 1 gm / ¼ tsp
Green coriander, chopped 30 gms / 2 tbs
Oil for frying

For the batter:

Gramflour *(besan)*, sifted 60 gms / 4 tbs
Cayenne pepper 1 gm / ¼ tsp
Salt 1 gm / ¼ tsp
Baking powder 1 gm / ¼ tsp
Water, cold 50 ml / ¼ cup

Method

1 Slice stems off the tomatoes, hollow out centres, drain upside down on a paper towel.

2 Knead cottage cheese and spices together. Fill each tomato cup with the mixture.

3 Mix the ingredients for the batter, adding water slowly. Whisk until batter is smooth and thick enough to seal in the filling and to evenly coat the tomatoes.

4 Dip each filled tomato in batter, coating evenly. Deep fry until golden brown on all sides. Remove, drain on paper towels. Serve hot.

BATTER COATED STUFFED TOMATOES

Serves: 6

Preparation time:
30-40 minutes

Cooking time: 30-40 minutes

Yam Kabab

Ingredients

Yam *(jimikand)* 1½ kg
Green chillies, finely chopped 5 gms / 1 tsp
Ginger, finely chopped 5 gms / 1 tsp
Salt 8 gms / 1½ tsp
White pepper powder 5 gms / 1 tsp
Red chilli powder 5 gms / 1 tsp
Chaat masala 5 gms / 1 tsp
Green coriander, finely chopped 5 gms / 1 tsp
Bread crumbs 100 gms / ½ cup
Oil 150 ml / ¾ cup

Method

1 Peel and wash the yam. Immerse in boiling water and cook until it becomes tender.

2 Remove from water, grate finely and squeeze out all cxccss water.

3 To the grated yam, add the remaining ingredients. Mix well and divide into 8 equal portions. Shape the portions into medallions.

4 Shallow fry each, on medium heat, till they become crisp and golden brown on both sides.

5 Serve hot, accompanied by Mint Chutney (page 102).

YAM KABAB

Serves: 4

Preparation time: 20 minutes

Cooking time: 20 minutes

Assorted Fritters

Ingredients

Gramflour (besan),
sifted 135 gms / 3/4 cup
Clarified butter (ghee) / Oil
+ for frying 10 ml / 2 tsp
Lemon juice 15 ml / 1 tbs
Cayenne pepper a pinch
Turmeric *(haldi)* powder a pinch
Garam masala (pg. 105) 5 gms / 1 tsp
Coriander powder 10 gms / 2 tsp
Salt 5 gms / 1 tsp
Water, cold 135 ml / 3/5 cup
Baking powder (optional) 3 gms / ½ tsp

Fritter suggestions:

Potatoes—cut into rounds
Cauliflower flowerets
Spinach—medium sized leaves
Green chillies—medium sized, slit lengthwise and filled with chaat masala
Cottage cheese (*paneer)—cut into 2" x 4" slices with chaat masala layered between 2 slices

Method

1 Combine together, the gramflour, clarified butter, lemon juice, cayenne pepper, turmeric powder, garam masala, ground coriander and salt. Mix well and add water (5 tbs). Whisk well to make batter lump-free. Slowly mix in more water till the consistency of batter resembles heavy cream and easily coats on the spoon.

2 Whisk again for about 3-5 minutes to further lighten the batter. Stir in baking powder if a cake-like crust is preferred.

3 Heat oil in a *kadhai* (wok) to upto 180 °C (335 °F).

4 Dip vegetables in the batter and slip one by one into the hot oil. Do not allow thefritters to stick to each other. Deep fry till the fritters are crisp and golden brown on each side.

5 Similarly, dip the cottage cheese sandwhich (with chaat masala filling) and the stuffed green chillies to coat evenly with the batter. Fry in the hot oil till crisp and golden brown on each side.

6 Serve hot, accompanied by Tomato Ketchup.

Assorted Fritters

Serves: 6

Preparation time: 10 minutes

Cooking time: 30 minutes

YOGHURT FLAVOURED, COTTAGE CHEESE CUTLETS

Ingredients

Cottage cheese *(paneer)*, finely grated
500 gms
Green cardamom *(choti elaichi)* powder
3 gms / ½ tsp
Egg white (optional) 1
Garam masala (pg. 105) 10 gms / 2 tsp
Green chillies, chopped 5 gms / 1 tsp
Green coriander, chopped 10 gms / 2 tsp
Mace powder *(javitri)* 3 gms / ½ tsp
Salt to taste
Onions, finely chopped 100 gms / ½ cup
Sesame *(til)* seeds (optional)
100 gms / ½ cup
White pepper powder 5 gms / 1 tsp
Yellow or red chilli powder
6 gms / 1 tsp
Yoghurt, hung 400 gms / 2 cups
Gramflour *(besan)* / Cornflour
60 gms / 4 tbs
Oil 100 ml / ½ cup

Method

1 Combine all the ingredients except the gram flour/cornflour, in a bowl. Mix with wooden spoon and season to taste.

2 Add the gram flour/cornflour and mix for 2 minutes.

3 Divide the mixture into 20 equal portions. Make each portion into a round ball, roll it in your palm and press slightly to get a 4 cm round patty.

4 Cool the patties in the refrigerator for 20 minutes.

5 Heat the oil in a deep pan or a *kadhai* (wok). Shallow fry in a nonstick pan until golden crisp. Alternatively, you could also lightly coat each patty with egg white.

6 Sprinkle with sesame seeds and shallow fry in a nonstick pan.

7 Serve with cucumber slices, tomato slices, onion slices and fresh Mint Chutney (page 102).

Yoghurt Flavoured, Cottage Cheese Cutlets

Serves: 4

Preparation: 30 minutes

Cooking: 15 minutes

Crispy Lentil Strips

Ingredients

Lentils *(chana daal)* 200 gms
Coriander seeds 15 gms / 1 tbs
Peppercorns 15 gms / 1 tbs
Ginger, chopped 10 gms / 2 tsp
Green coriander, chopped 15 gms /1 tbs
Green chillies, chopped 2
Salt to taste
Red chilli powder 5 gms / 1 tsp
Garam masala (pg. 105) 5 gms / 1 tsp
Oil for frying

Method

1 Soak lentils for 4-5 hours or in warm water for ½ hour. Drain and blend alongwith coriander seeds and pepper corns to make a coarsely ground thick paste.

2 Put the paste into a big bowl and add the remaining ingredients, mix thoroughly and keep aside for 30 minutes.

3 Heat oil in a *kadhai* (wok) till it is smoking. Moisten hands and shape the mixture into 10 cm flat patties. Fry patties for 2-3 minutes on both sides and remove from oil. Drain excess oil and allow to cool.

4 Slice the patties into 3-4 strips. Reheat oil till smoking, lower heat to medium and fry the strips till they are crisp and golden brown on both sides. Drain excess oil and serve hot, accompanied by Mint Chutney (page 102).

CRISPY LENTIL STRIPS

Serves: 4-6

Preparation time: 5-6 hours

Cooking time: 30 minutes

Brown onion paste

Ginger-garlic paste

Green chilli paste

Meal for Two

Soup
Cold Cucumber Soup 8
Main Course
Fish Rolls 76
Cottage Cheese and Capsicum Delight 78
Accompaniments
Khasta Roti 86
Mushroom Pulao 20
Dessert
Kesar Sandesh 70

Soup
Tomato and Coriander Soup 20
Starter
Tandoori Salad 70
Main Course
Chicken with Spinach 10
Tangy Aubergines 102
Accompaniments
Khameeri Roti 28
Lemon Rice 12
Dessert
Rasgoola 54

Soup
Carrot and Orange Soup 14

Starter
Prawn Cutlet 60
Main Course
Goan Fish Curry 70
Mushrooms in Tomato Gravy 88
Accompaniment
Stuffed Parantha 36
Dessert
Shahi Tukda Nawabi 66

Soup
Tomato and Coconut Soup 16
Main Course
Chicken with Black Pepper 20
Spiced Cauliflower 94
Accompaniments
Daal Makhani 40
Cottage Cheese Pulao 22
Khameeri Roti 38
Dessert
Rajbhog 56

Starter
Chicken Spring Roll 32
Potato Baskets 90
Main Course
Lamb Curry 52
Accompaniments
Mint Raita 94
Tandoori Roti 38

For vegetarian

Soup
Spinach Soup 12
Starter
Cottage Cheese Tikka 80
Main Course
Tangy Gramflour Curry 46
Accompaniment
Khasta Roti 86
Dessert
Kheer 78

Brunches

Starters
Potato Baskets 90
Prawn Cutlets 60
Main Course
Stir-fried Chicken with Spring Onions 26
Accompaniments
Mint Chutney 102
Lachha Parantha 32
Dessert
Moong Daal Halwa 76

Starters
Assorted Fritters 98
Fish Rolls stuffed with Prawns 68
Main Course
Minced Lamb with Peas 36
Stir-fried Mushrooms 86
Accompaniments
Poori 24
Tomato Chutney 100
Dessert
Malpua 64

Soup
Spinach soup 12
Starters
Cauliflower Kabab 78

Crispy Lentil Strips 102
Main Course
Fenugreek flavoured Prawns 58
Stir-fried Lamb Delight 46
Accompaniments
Tandoori Roti 38
Orange Raita 98
Dessert
Rabari 88

Soup
Tomato and Coriander Soup 20
Starters
Stuffed Cottage Cheese Tikka 84
Tomatoes stuffed with Mushroom 92
Main Course
Crispy Cauliflower 96
Lamb Curry 52
Accompaniment
Khameeri Roti 28
Dessert
Gulab Jamum 50

Soup
Exotic Lamb Soup 10
Main Course
Tomato flavoured Chicken 12
Spicy Lamb Chops 40
Accompaniment
Daal Makhani 40
Khameeri Roti 28
Naan 34
Dessert
Kheer 78

For vegetarian

Starters
Cottage Cheese Croquettes 82
Yam Kabab 96
Main Course
Crunchy Okra 92
Minced Peas and Potatoes 98
Accompaniment
Khasta Roti 86
Dessert
Gajrela 74

List of Indian Spices

Amchoor (*Dried mango powder*): Amchoor gives foods a slight sourness. Lemon juice may be substituted.

Aniseed (*Sweet cumin*): Aromatic seeds used in meat dishes. Also eaten as a digestive after meals.

Asafoetida (*Heeng*): A pungent grainy powder used mainly for its digestive properties.

Bay leaf (*Tej patta*): An aromatic herb used for flavouring vegetable and meat dishes.

Cardamom, green (*Choti elaichi*): An aromatic spice, generally sold in its pod; used whole in pods or with its seeds ground.

Cardamom, large black (*Badi elaichi*): A spice, used in many vegetable and meat dishes. The black pods are ground whole.

Carom seeds (*Ajwain*): Also known as thymol or omum seeds; used in pickles and vegetable dishes.

Chillies, whole dried red (*Sabut lal mirch*): Used like the green chillies but much hotter.

Cinnamon (*Dalchini*): Available in powder or stick form; used in curries and pulaos.

Cloves (*Laung*): Dried flower buds, available whole or ground; used in savouries and for pickling.

Coriander seeds, whole/ground (*Dhania*): Seeds of the coriander plant. Available as whole seeds or powdered form.

Cumin seeds (*Jeera*): Available as whole seeds or powdered.

Cumin seeds (*Shah jeera*): A caraway-like seed with a flavour that is more subtle than that of ordinary cumin; to be used in small quantities.

Curry leaves, fresh and dried (*Kari patta*): Highly aromatic leaves, shaped like small bay leaves. Use fresh leaves or the less aromatic dried ones.

Fennel seeds (*Saunf*): These seeds are larger but look and taste like aniseeds.

Fenugreek seeds (*Methi*): Yellow, square and flat, the seeds have a slightly bitter flavour.

Kasoori methi (*Fenugreek leaves, dried*): A rare herb grown in the Kasoor region of Pakistan. The dried leaves, readily available in handy packets, are largely used in chicken and lamb preparations to give the dishes a sweet aroma.

Mace (*Javitri*): The outer membrane of nutmeg, with a similar taste; available as blades or powder. Used in meat dishes.

Melon seeds (*Magaz*): Peeled melon seeds are used in savoury dishes.

Mustard seeds, whole black (*Sarson*): Tiny dark round seeds, black or reddish-brown. Used for tempering in daals and pickles.

Nutmeg (*Jaiphal*): Used grated or ground, for flavouring sweets and savouries.

Onion seeds (*Kalonji*): Sprinkled over Indian oven breads and used in cooking vegetables and fish.

Pomegranate seeds (*Anardana*): Seeds used in making savouries, and for flavouring.

Poppy seeds (*Khus khus*): Tiny white seeds.

Red chilli powder (*Pisi hui lal mirch*): Ground dried red chillies. The nearest equivalent is red cayenne pepper powder.

Turmeric (*Haldi*): Yellow, powdered spice, used for colouring and flavouring.

Ajwain (Carom seeds)

Amchur (Green mango powder)

Bari elaichi (Black cardamom)

Choti elaichi (Green cardamom)

Dhania (Coriander powder)

Daalchini (Cinnamon sticks)

Haldi (Turmeric powder)

Heeng (Asafoetida)

Javitri (mace)

Kali mirch (Black pepper corn)

Khus khus (Poppy seeds)

Laung (Cloves)

Lal mirch (Red chilli)

Methidana (Fenugreek seeds)

Raee (Mustard seeds)

Basic Indian Recipes

Brown onion paste:
Slice onions (500 gms) and fry over medium heat until brown. Remove drain excess oil and allow to cool. Process until pulped, using very little water if required. Remove to an air tight container and refrigerate. Use as and when required.

Garam masala:
(For 450 gms), broil the following ingredients in a thick bottomed pan, cumin seeds (200 gms), black peppercorn (35 gms), black cardamom seeds (45 gms), green cardamom (30 gms), coriander seeds (60 gms), cloves (20 gms) communion stick (20 gms), mace powder (20 gms), bay leaves (15 gms), ginger powder (30 gms) and Nutmeg (2). Allow to cool and grind to a powder. Store in an air tight container and use as required.

Ginger/Garlic paste:
Soak ginger/garlic (300 gms) overnight to soften the skin. Peel and chop roughly and process until pulped. Remove to an air tight container and store in a refrigerator. Use as and when required.

Green Chilli paste:
Take required quantity of green chillies, chop roughly and process until pulped.

Khoya:
Boil milk (2 liters) in a kadhai (wok). Reduce heat and cook till quantity reduces to half, stirring occasionally continue cooking, now stirring constantly and scraping from all sides, till a thick paste-like consistency is obtained (1-1½ hrs). Allow to cool.

Onion paste:
Peel and chop onions (500 gms) in quarters and process until pulped. Remove in an air tight container and refrigerate. Use as and when required.

Paneer (*Cottage cheese*):
In a pot, put milk (3 litres) to boil. Just before it boils add lemon juice or white vinegar (60 ml / 4 tbs) to curdle the milk. Strain the curdled milk through a cushion cloth to allow all whey and moisture to drain. Allow to hang under a weight for 2-3 hours to set in a block which can be cut or grated.

Red Chilli paste:
Take required quantity of green chillies, chop roughly and process until pulped.

Tomato Purée:
Peel and chop the tomatoes (1 kg), remove the seeds. In a pan, cook the tomatoes on medium heat alongwith water (1 litre), cloves 8, green cardamom 8, ginger 15 gms, garlic 10 gms, bay leaves 5 and black peppercorns 5 gms, until the tomatoes are tender. Remove from heat, allow to cool and process until pulped. Store in an air tight container. Use as and when required.